This book belongs to

Marilyn Hoeppner

Preparing for Jesus

Books by Walter Wangerin Jr.

The Book of God: The Bible as a Novel
The Book of the Dun Cow
The Book of Sorrows
Little Lamb, Who Made Thee?
The Manger Is Empty
Miz Lil and the Chronicles of Grace
Mourning Into Dancing
The Orphean Passages
Ragman and Other Cries of Faith
Reliving the Passion
Whole Prayer

For Children

Mary's First Christmas
Peter's First Easter
The Book of God for Children

WALTER
WANGERIN JR.

Preparing for Jesus

Meditations
on the
Coming *of* Christ,
Advent,
Christmas,
and the
Kingdom

ZondervanPublishingHouse
Grand Rapids, Michigan

A Division of HarperCollins*Publishers*

Preparing for Jesus
Copyright © 1999 by Walter Wangerin Jr.

Requests for information should be addressed to:

 ZondervanPublishingHouse
Grand Rapids, Michigan 49530

Library of Congress Cataloging-in-Publication Data

Wangerin, Walter.
    Preparing for Jesus : meditations on the coming of Christ, Advent,
  Christmas, and the Kingdom / Walter Wangerin, Jr.
        p. cm.
    Includes bibliographical references.
    ISBN 0-310-20644-8
    1. Advent Meditations. 2. Christmas Meditations. I. Title.
  BV40.W29 1999
  242'.33—dc21   99-35510
                                                              CIP

This edition printed on acid-free paper.

All Scripture quotations, unless otherwise indicated, are taken from the
Revised Standard Version or from the author's own paraphrase.

Published in association with the literary agency of Alive Communications,
Inc., 1465 Kelly Johnson Blvd. #320, Colorado Springs, CO 80920.

Interior design by Nancy Wilson

Printed in the United States of America

99 00 01 02 03 04 05 /❖ DC/ 10 9 8 7 6 5 4 3 2 1

To Paul,
brother of unbroken love
and loyalty

CONTENTS

PART FOUR:
Elizabeth

PART FIVE:
John

PART SIX:
Joseph

PART SEVEN:
Jesus

PREFACE

THROUGHOUT MY LIFE it has been my good fortune to experience the story of Jesus with every turning of every year. The number of the years of my unfolding age is also the number of times I've traveled with my Lord from his birth to his death to his triumphant rising again.

And because the story has been more than *told* to me; because it has *surrounded* me like a weather; because it *comprehends* me as a house does its inhabitants or a mother does her child, the life of Christ has shaped mine. My very being has been molded in him.

And because my response to this story has been more than an act of mind, more than study and scrutiny; because the story invites my entering in and my personal participation; because I have *experienced* the life of Christ with deeper intensity than I have my own daily affairs, the Gospel story now interprets for me the world's story. It is through the Gospel narrative, as through a window or a template, that I see all things, that I relate to them and come to know them.

In every sense of the phrase: I find myself in Jesus.

As I enter his story, I enter him. As his life embraces mine, he embraces me, and I am his.

But how has this story come to me with such size and force these fifty-five years?

11

No single person has been responsible, nor only the people of this present age. Rather, it is the gift of a vast communion of worshiping Christians, saints of many ages, many lands, and many tongues, countless talents all expressing the one faith founded upon the life of Christ.

It is the gift of the church, ancient and contemporary.

For the church past has bequeathed to the church present a grand theatric—a drama, as it were—which takes six months to enact, December into May. There is no audience. All are actors. And *this* play, rather than representing something different from itself, actually contains and communicates the truth, for its protagonist is the Lord Jesus, and the Lord is always present in his Word—and the Lord *is* truth.

In my own ecclesiastic tradition, this divine drama is given conscious focus in our worship services. Each Sunday's service involves all the people in a new episode of the story of the life of Christ.

Involves the people: for the Bible readings bring before us new details and the holy affirmation that this is, wholly and in all its part, the Word of God. And music persuades our mood, our emotions, and our voices to join. And preaching elaborates. And the building itself becomes a stage arranged with symbolic furniture for serious action, water washings, eatings and drinkings, risings and fallings. But even as the drama is real, so is this "stage" a real meeting place between the hero and the rest of the players— between, that is, the Christ, and the Christians who have not come as a passive audience, but as actors uttering their (real!) lines in song and prayer, in creed and spontaneous expressions of sorrow or joy: *Amen! Hallelujah!*

∽

Each Sunday's service, as I've said, involves the people in a new episode; but altogether all the Sundays weave the entire drama of Jesus into something like five acts.

I have been one of those people so fiercely involved. This is the way that I've been shaped. And these are the acts that have driven my whole person so dramatically close to Jesus:

Act 1: *Advent*

Before the hero enters, people anticipate his coming. Old promises are remembered. New promises are made. Excitement sparks and burns in the hearts of all the players: Zechariah, Elizabeth, Mary, Joseph, you, me, the children. Daily the excitement blazes hotter and hotter until we can scarcely stand it.

Who's coming? What's his name? What'll he be like? What's he going to do?

People prepare. Christians examine themselves. They clean up their lives, interior and exterior, making themselves ready to meet the hero at his coming. So kindled are many emotions that good hearts break into song both in heaven and on earth, waiting, waiting for . . .

Act 2: *Christmas*

Enter the hero . . . as a baby! No, not in power nor in any trappings of royalty or heroism that the world can recognize, but exactly as any one of us has come, weak and needy—though the angels sing and the heavens conjoin in one bright, declarative light.

The event itself—this divine, completely human birth—occupies the attentions of all players, parents and shepherds and evangelists and you and me and the children.

We rejoice.

Act 3: *Epiphany*

Time to meet the hero, discover what sort of person he is and why he's come.

On the day of Epiphany itself we make our meeting by joining the Magi of the East. Ah, this is what he is: he's a king after all, deserving of worship, but not a king like Herod wielding power.

The Sundays of this third act continue in verbal explanations and in wonderful events to reveal the character and the nature of Jesus: baptized the Son of God, a teacher both sublime and confident of this own authority, a miracle worker, and yet again, when his face ignites like the sun, the beloved Son of God.

We marvel.

Act 4: *Lent*

And now the hero goes to work. Conflict is engaged. Christ, wholly human and altogether divine, encounters Satan and sin and sickness and ignorance and death. He tells us what is to happen to him (though we, with Peter, resist the plan, unable to accept his suffering and his dying). Forces spiritual and political rise up against him. Tensions grow impossible. Conflict increases. Something, something is about to happen. . . .

Then all horrors refine themselves into a terrible simplicity as we with Jesus suffer the climax of the story, of his life and of our Gospel: during that one week called "Holy" we suffer with the sufferings of Jesus, the Thursday night of his new commandment, the Friday when he dies, the Saturday of unutterable gloom.

Oh, no! The play cannot end here, can it? If the story of Jesus ends now, so must all meaning in the world and all hope. Our faith would be in vain.

Act 5: *Easter*

But Sunday explodes with an altogether different climax! Whereas Good Friday was dark, Easter Sunday is bright with divine laughter and a life that death cannot destroy.

Jesus rises from the dead.

We who died with him are granted blazing proofs that we shall also rise with him.

And this particular Sunday is only the first of his act, for now we follow the risen hero as he makes himself apparent to many disciples—and we ourselves experience the effect of these appearings, for the disciples then represent Christians now.

Forty days later (as Luke counted the days of Jesus on earth, and as our drama enacts them) we gather to watch Jesus ascend to the right hand of the Father, promising yet to return for us.

And on the final day of this act, the final day of the whole play, the fiftieth day since Jesus arose and the tenth since he ascended, we gather again with the apostles on Pentecost. Can you hear the wind? Do you see the tongues of flame on the heads of those to utter the Word, who proclaim the Gospel, who tell the story again this year? Of course.

And with the Holy Spirit at Pentecost comes down as well a responsibility upon the whole Church: to continue the work of Jesus upon the earth. Therefore, the following six months (June through November) pay attention to what *we,* the followers of Jesus, must be, and what *we* must do, and how our lives must develop even through death to life again.

Several years ago—in order to share with you this *experience* of the story of Jesus—I wrote a book of meditations for the climatic third act of the divine drama: Lent. I entitled that book, *Reliving the Passion*.

Now I offer you another book of meditations, this one for the first and second acts of the drama: Advent and Christmas.

As the first book ended with one day of Easter, so this will end with one day of Epiphany.

In both cases it is my suggestion that you read one meditation for each day of the season.

With this book, schedule your readings according to the calendar, beginning on December 1 and concluding on January 6, which is the twelfth day of Christmas (according to western liturgies), and is also the day of the Epiphany itself.

Please note:

The meditations of this book will vary one from another. In some I will speak directly to you as your pastor, your teacher, your friend. In others I will carry you into the story by speaking to biblical characters. Sometimes I will imagine the details, the historical events in the story, and tell it objectively. At other times I'll tell the story glancingly, in order to make direct application to our lives.

Be prepared, then, for changes as you begin each new day's dialogue between me and you.

It is my intent to create for you a richness in devotional variety which is equal to the richness of yourself. For you are as complex as the church that has preserved the story of Jesus. You think. You study. You breathe and feel and smile. You bite your lip. You observe from a cool distance, then suddenly you react with a subjective passion. You love. You act in evident relationship with other people, *and* you act invisibly, in the chambers of your heart, in spirit, in Jesus.

As you, my friend, are a various being, so these meditations—in order to involve the greater part of you in the story—shall be various too.

Peace to you, and power upon your experience of our coming King.

Walt Wangerin

PART ONE

Prepare

A Teaching:
Four Questions for the Final Advent

MARK 13:32–37:

> *Jesus said, "But of that day or that hour no one knows, not even the angels in heaven, nor the Son, but only the Father. Take heed. Watch—for you do not know when the time will come. It is like a man going on a journey, when he leaves home and puts his servants in charge, each with his work, and commands the doorkeeper to be on the watch.*
>
> *"Watch, therefore, for you do not know when the master of the house will come, in the evening, or at midnight, or at cockcrow, on in the morning.*
>
> *"Watch, lest he come suddenly and find you asleep.*
>
> *"And what I say to you I say to all: Watch."*

T HE WORD ADVENT is derived from the Latin *adventus*, which means "the approach" or "the arrival." The verb is *advenio*: "I arrive. I come. I am coming."

Who is coming?

As a season of the Christian year, Advent is ancient. It goes back at least to the middle of the sixth century. Already then its observance defined not only the One who was coming, but also those who were faithfully and self-consciously waiting. It defined the peculiar *people* who looked forward to the coming of that One.

Who is coming? *Who awaits him?*

By the thirteenth century, the Church universal had recognized the season of Advent as the beginning of its year. Advent consisted of four Sundays, the first of which was New Year's Day for Christians everywhere—and so it was that Advent also defined the *times*, endings and beginnings, the past and the present, as well as the future when the Blessed One would come.

Who is coming? Who awaits him? And *when will he get here?*

For nearly one thousand five hundred years Christians have spent the days of Advent not in passive inaction, but in activities strenuous and profitable: they have *prepared* themselves by scrubbing and cleaning their lives, by examining and repairing their souls—even as people generally prepare themselves body and home to receive a visitor of ineffable importance.

Who is coming? Who awaits him? When will he get here? And *how shall the people prepare?*

The Son of man, *he* is coming. Jesus. That one. Him.

And we are the people who await him. You and I. Since it was for us he died, *we* are the ones who wait in love. And since he ascended to heaven with promises to return, we wait in faith—for at the next and final Advent, Jesus will take us as friends, as brothers and sisters into his house forevermore.

And when will he get here? Like any New Year's Day: at the end and the beginning.

But that Advent to come—the final arrival of Jesus in glory—will itself *cause* the end of this present age and the beginning of our eternal joy. When will that be? Ah, my friend, I do not know. No one knows its day or hour. Therefore Jesus commands us to "Watch. Stay awake. Get ready. Prepare, prepare—and watch!"

Finally, then, how shall we prepare? In *these* days, while yet there are days and time, by what activity should we make ourselves ready?

Why, by meditating on his first coming—for though the future may be hidden from us the past is not, and the one can teach us the other.

The story of the birth of Jesus is open before us. We have a spiritual and holy account of the time when God himself directed preparations for that first coming of his Son into the world. What God ordains is always good. Therefore, *those* preparations may be the perfect pattern for our own this year again, this year too.

Behold, I bring you good news of great joy! The people who heard the news of that first Advent were no less human than we. They moved through complex stages of response: doubt, fear, questioning, the obedience of love, the obedience of legalism, joy and song, despair and anger. There were groups of people, shepherds, the Magi, innocent children; there were individuals, Zachariah, Elizabeth, Mary, Joseph, Simeon, Anna, Herod. Some concluded their preparations in faith. Some in fury. Any one of these might be you, my friend. Or me. But we have the advantage, now, of meditation: in quietness and confidence to choose the right response, and, by the grace of the present Spirit of Jesus, to practice the right preparation for the coming of the Lord in Glory.

So let us enter the story one more time. In this present season of Advent let us experience the infant's Advent in the past and so make ourselves ready for the Advent of the Lord of Glory in the future.

O Lord,

Stir up, we beg you, your power—and come. Come even now into this season of our meditations, that by your protection we may be rescued from our sins, and saved by your mighty deliverance in order to look forward to your final arrival with the joy that cannot be uttered. We pray in your name, O Lord, for you live and reign with the Father and the Holy Spirit, one God, now and forever.

Amen

PART TWO

Zechariah

A Consolation:
You Are Not Little in the Universe

LUKE 1:5–7:

> *In the days of Herod, king of Judea, there was a certain priest named Zechariah who belonged to the division of Abijah. He had a wife descended from Aaron. Her name was Elizabeth. They were both righteous in God's sight, observing all the commandments and ordinances of the Lord without the least blame.*
>
> *Nevertheless, they had no children because Elizabeth was barren. They were very old.*

EVERY PRESENT MOMENT is well-rooted in the past. Nothing happens in pure isolation. No human is so alienated that he has no history or so lonesome that she cannot find life lines through which her person has emerged. We are never only *I*. We are always, somehow, *we*.

Even the miracles of God, so sudden-seeming, have been nurtured in love through the ages to the moment of their appearing. But it may be only *in* the appearing that God's careful tending of this thing is made clear to us.

God, you see, is God of history: weaving its past and its future together; designing the times by overseeing the intricate patterns of human events; granting meaning to the whole of humankind, and thereby making any single moment, also, incandescent with meaning.

∞

Even so did God prepare for the entrance of the Savior into the world.

Even so, in Luke, do these few verses about one humble old man indicate: the past, the entire past of human need and divine desire, is spiraling into Judea to produce this drama of the coming of the infant Jesus. Jesus!—who shall himself illuminate the whole history of humankind with a fearful and beautiful meaning.

—For the old man's name is Zechariah—and he is scarcely the first to bear that name in Israel. Scripture records thirty Zechariahs before him, kings and prophets and priests and Levites. He is the fruit of an ancient family tree, himself a priest, his wife a Levite.

—For the old man's name itself means: *Yahweh remembers.* God is remembering his people, yes. But the divine act of remembering is in fact the containing of all things past in God's awareness, shaping the past presently, in this present calling to mind. God remembers now, and all that was exists even now in his mind!

—For God is remembering, too, his promises, his most ancient promises. And this is signified in the circumstances of Zechariah and his wife, Elizabeth; for they cause our first parents, Abraham and Sarah, to be present again. Zechariah and Elizabeth represent that ancient couple unto whom God promised: "In you all the families of the earth shall be blessed" (Gen. 12:3b).

In all of Scripture, these are the only couples both childless *and* too old to bear children; and in only these two cases does God announce the improbable birth not to the mother, but to the father. Therefore, Abraham and Sarah once introduced a fresh covenant between God and the earth, so Zechariah and Elizabeth now introduce the final covenant of grace, and the lines between them run unbroken—for no other reason than that the love of God did not break against human sin!

You see? All history is, like a woman in labor, concentrating on this single, central event: the coming of the Son of God among us.

—For now, *now* the "remembering" of his promises means also that God is keeping them, physically, in human time and human space, and in the sight of every people.

So here you are, my friend—this year, this day, this particular moment—bowed down in meditations and preparing for the coming of the Lord. This tick in your Advent clock: how insignificant it seems in the order of things, yes?

But it isn't—and you are not—insignificant at all! Surely you have taken the lesson of these verses: how vast and complex is the history that brings you *to* this moment! How countless the divine preparations that presently shape your meditation! Not only do you, your personhood, your *self*, derive from the bloodlines of your ancestors; not only does the more immediate history of your culture shape your days and ways; but the flower of this moment has a root as deep in antiquity as the time when God spoke promises to Abraham and Sarah. And its sunshine is Christ! For the birth of that light into the world (an event midway between Abraham and you) illumines all our human history, making this particular moment, too, incandescent with meaning.

Did you think you were little in the universe? Ah, but look how God has used the universe to bring you here. Like any miracle of God, you have been nurtured in love through all the ages unto this instant, this breath you now are drawing, this present beating of your heart, this thought, this faith, this prayer....

O Lord,

Catch us up, like Zechariah, in the whirl of your holy history. We seem to be but particles in the wind; but you declare each one of us to be a particular person, spokes in the great wheel of your covenant-loving of the world.

Let us be meek in your kingdom, but not abject; humble, not self-pitiful; obedient, not obsequious; servants, not servile; childlike, not childish; yours in love and willingness, and then our smallness shall be your greatness indeed.

Amen

O Zechariah:
How Did It Feel Meeting Glory Face to Face?

LUKE 1:8–13A:

> *Now, while Zechariah was serving as priest, during the time his division was on Temple duty in God's presence, lots were cast according to the priesthood, and it fell to him to enter the sanctuary of the Lord to burn the incense.*
>
> *At this hour of incense, the whole multitude of the people were praying outside.*
>
> *And there appeared to Zechariah an angel of the Lord, standing at the right side of the altar of incense. As soon as he saw the angel, he was struck with confusion and fear.*
>
> *But the angel said to him, "Zechariah, don't be afraid ..."*

OLD MAN, GREY MAN, how did it feel that afternoon, so to be whipsawed by events—cut high and low, torn from delight to disaster and death?

Oh, God is a wind, and God is a whirlwind when we meet him.

1. First, the servant's labor:

How many years, twice a year, had you traveled to Jerusalem to perform the duties of your priesthood? Many years. You are old. Was there honor in the job? Some. Not much, seeing there were 18,000 other priests and Levites in Palestine. Honor for you was what you gave to the Lord by your service. Not high, not low your experience, then, but steadfast in its obedience.

And on that morning, as on every other morning, your priestly division cast lots to see who would serve in four particular capacities that day: one to offer burnt offering, one to offer the meal offering, one to care for the candlestick in the Sanctuary—and one to offer incense. The first three duties carried a certain prestige, indeed. But the fourth was the most honorable of all. No priest, having offered incense once, could do it again—until the rest of the priests had each had his chance. You, old man—you had never done it. Nor did any lot fall to you that morning either.

So how did the day feel at its beginning? Common. Unremarkable.

2. Then the breakthrough:

That afternoon only one lot was cast, one duty only assigned: that of offering the evening incense.

Zechariah, it fell to you!

All at once you were called to one of the highest celebrations of your professional life! The first time and the last time, too. And you loved the Lord before whom priests burned incense morning and evening, a perpetual fragrance throughout your generations.

Oh, with what delight you vested yourself for the ceremony!

Did you even *see* the people gathering in the courtyard?

Old man, did your legs shiver as you walked between two assistants into the sanctuary of the Temple? One assistant opened a silver firepan and poured bright coals onto the altar. The other set a dish of incense at its side. They both withdrew, and you were left alone.

Did your hand tremble when you took the silver spoon and scooped a little dark powder, the fragrance waiting its release? Did your heart kick at the honor?—for you alone in all Israel were making ready the prayers of the people, the delight of the Lord, the most holy thing you've done in all your life!

But however high this office, it was not unfamiliar to you; you had imagined it a thousand times. The next thing, however—that thing was unimaginable altogether.

3. The holy terror, the glory:

Just as the incense touched the coals and sparkled and breathed a sweet white smoke into the air, the very curtain of creation ripped asunder! Matter tore open, and the immaterial arrived so brightly beside you that your heart stopped.

Behold: at the right side of the altar stood the angel of the Lord. How did *that* feel? How, at the blazing intrusion of Heaven, did your earthly person react? Could you breathe? Was your face flaming? Were your limbs frozen, mortally cold? Did you feel as if you had died?

Well, yes: dying was precisely the fear of certain high priests when they entered the Holy of Holies, for God had said to Moses: *You cannot see my face; no one can see me and live* (Ex. 33:20). The glory of the Lord could strike a human dead; and who could pull him out of that elemental darkness then, when none *but* the High Priest could ever enter there?

Old man, your hand at the incense, your body bombed by God!

Every common thing in your world was blown away.

Professional choices, the priesthood with all its duties and even its highest honors, turned to ashes in this uncreated light.

Time and space and human experience were rendered meaningless.

Yes, yes, in the presence of the glory of the Holy One, it was as if you were truly dead.

4. Resurrection, the same glory:

But then the glory that had reduced you to plain mortality, by whose bright contrast you were revealed as dust— that same celestial intrusion spoke in a language you could understand.

Zechariah, it said. It uttered your name! Your person, your identity, your very self were given presence and form in the voice of the glory of God.

And Glory said, *Zechariah, don't be afraid.*

Then what? Glory surrounded you with comfort. Then how did you feel?

Isn't it a wonder, father Zechariah, that the mere presence of the divine destroys our sinful selves and all we thought defined us, but that the *Word* of the divine consoles us, relieves us, forgives us, and raises us up again?

This is the very paradox of God; and you, old man, are its paradigm, since the four-part sequence of your experience is like our own: neither common life nor the best of life sustain us; and God, when we encounter him, seems first to do us violence; but the violence is in fact benevolence to us, for God is destroying false gods in order to prepare us to receive him as God alone, and his mercy as the very core of our existence.

How does it feel, old man? After all these years, how does it feel to be a baby again?

O Father of our Lord Jesus
and, by him, Father of ourselves,
when you see that the world is too much with us
(some—you must see for us, since that same world
blinds us to our real conditions) rouse us. Stir up our
hearts. Let heaven intrude upon our earthly affairs to
rip our attentions from the world to you again.
Christmas is such an intrusion.
At Christmas heaven invaded the world.
Immanuel Jesus caused the fall and the rising of
many. Even so do we pray that Immanuel would
frighten and free us, too.

Amen

A Teaching:
How God Enlarges Little Prayers

LUKE 1:13–17:

> But the angel said to him, "Zechariah, don't be afraid, for your prayer is heard:
>
> Your wife Elizabeth will bear you a son,
> and you will call his name John.
> You will have joy and gladness,
> and many will rejoice at his birth.
>
> For he will be great before the Lord,
> and he will drink no wine or strong drink.
> And he will be filled with the Holy Spirit even
>   from his mother's womb,
> and he will turn many of the sons of Israel to the
>   Lord their God.
>
> He will go before Him
> in the spirit and power of Elijah
> to turn the hearts of fathers to their children
> and the disobedient unto the wisdom of the just,
> to make ready for the Lord a people prepared."

ONE NIGHT in the dead of winter a woman entered the room of her small son and paused to tip her head and listen.

When she heard how painful and labored his breathing was, she fell on her knees beside him and wept and prayed.

"Save his life, save his life," she prayed.

The little boy had asthma. His mother had often heard this troubled respiration, and had often prayed this prayer. But on this particular night she was also exhausted, and that's why she wept when she prayed: "Save his life. O Lord, possess his life. Use his life for something good and then you will have good reason to let him live a long life in this world. Please, please, save his life."

By morning the boy's breathing was better—as was usual after a difficult night.

By the time he reached adolescence, the boy himself was better. It isn't unusual for children to outgrow asthmatic conditions during puberty and never suffer them again.

By the time he was an adult, the boy's mother had forgotten the prayer she had prayed so many years before.

But God had not forgotten. God does not forget.

Long, long after that cold midwinter night when his mother had given him to God that God might give him life, the man met Jesus on the road between two cities and this was the real crisis of his life, his fierce conversion, the beginning of a lifelong ministry ... and the answer to his mother's prayer.

Such is the love of God, both for those who pray, and for those prayed over, *and* for the whole world altogether, which receives the benefit of the prayer and of its answer.

For what if that mother's son was named, in Hebrew, Saul? And in Greek, Paul? Or maybe the name of that mother's son was something of a sillier sound, like Wally.

∞

Who knows when Zechariah and Elizabeth prayed the prayer the angel mentions? Surely it was long ago, before they had grown old. The prayer was a plea to bear children, of course, so it must have begun soon after they had married. It must have grown more anguished as longer and longer grew the time when God did *not* answer it. But after a certain age reality must have persuaded the childless couple to stop praying for the impossible.

By now they had probably forgotten the prayer itself. Surely they believed that its purpose was past—and that the answer long, long ago had been, "No."

But here is the first of our lessons today: that God does not forget our prayers. It is in the fullness of time that he answers them. He answers in that rich *kairos*, when to answer at all does the most good for the most people!

And that is the second lesson: that the particular and seeming-private prayer becomes, in God's omnipotent answer, a universal benefaction. Universal: something for all flesh, something that binds all time together.

And you, my friend—you thought your older prayers had gone unanswered (because we live always in the particular present, forgetting the past, unknowing the future).

And you thought your personal praying had nothing to do with anyone besides yourself and a handful of intimate folk (because our own vision is confined to a particular space, place, community).

But your prayer is never yours alone. It is also God's, you know.

∞

So the young couple prayed for a baby.

And in the fullness of time, yes, God gave it to them.

But the child they wanted was also the man God wanted, and what the Lord gave to that particular couple he also gave to the world: a prophet filled with the Holy Spirit! Another Elijah! A "messenger" to prepare a people for the coming of the Lord.

"You shall call his name *John*," which in Hebrew is *Yeho-hanan* or *Yohanan*. It means "Yahweh has given grace."

Oh, what a vast answer to tiny praying! Grace for two becomes grace for the whole world!

And look how all time is also completely embraced in this answer: the *past* is fulfilled in this Spiritual child, that the *future* might still hear his message and prepare to receive the Lord.

Time past? "Behold," said the Lord through Malachi (long before the young couple married, met, or even appeared on earth): "I send my messenger to prepare the way before me, and the Lord whom you seek will suddenly come to his temple; the messenger of the covenant in whom you delight, behold, he is coming"(3:1).

And again, "Behold, I will send you Elijah the prophet, before the great and terrible day of the Lord comes. And he will turn the hearts of the fathers to their children, and the hearts of the children to their fathers, lest I come and smite the land with a curse"(4:5–6—the very last words of the Old Testament).

Of course these past prophecies are familiar. The angel repeats them in order to describe the mighty work that John will do to prepare for the coming of the Lord Jesus: John is as Elijah was, accomplishing now what the prophets proclaimed; past is present.

And the future? Well, the angel's repetition of old promises makes them new promises *for* the future, for the lifetime of John, and then for every next generation which must "turn . . . to the Lord our God," every one of us who even today "prepares" for the coming of the Lord.

So now, my friend, you are about to pray a little prayer. Whom shall you pray for? What is your immediate heart's desire? Pray it. Use simple words. Consider but your own plain portion of existence. It is enough. It is good and fully enough. For even as you pray it, the prayer lodges with God—eternal, omnipotent, God only wise—never to die but in the fullness of time to find its holiest, most blessed expression.

Let us, each in our own words, pray the personal prayer . . .

Amen

DECEMBER FIVE

An Exhortation:
Trust God, and His Signs Will Delight You

LUKE 1:18–23:

> *But Zechariah said to the angel, "How shall I know this? I am an old man, and my wife is advanced in years."*
>
> *The angel answered, "I am Gabriel. I stand in the presence of God! I was sent to speak to you and to tell you this good news. Behold, because you did not believe my words, you will be silent, unable to speak until the day these things actually happen, which they will! My words shall certainly be fulfilled."*
>
> *The people waiting for Zechariah began to wonder at his delay in the temple. When he did come out, he couldn't speak to them, so they perceived that he had seen a vision in the sanctuary. He made signs to them.*
>
> *He remained mute during the rest of his service at the temple and even when he went home again.*

WHEN IN DELIGHT I ask for a sign by which to remember some sweet promise, the sign itself becomes a keepsake, a treasure among my possessions. It reflects both the trust of the promisee and the trustworthiness of the promisor.

When in doubt I demand a sign as proof that a certain promise can and will be kept, *that* sign becomes a cold legality, a contract, a bond that binds the promisor. It reflects the mistrust of the promisee, the presumption of fault in the promisor.

Thirty years ago my wife and I made foundational promises each to the other: to be faithful unto death. This is not a merely sentimental thing. It is absolutely the ground upon which we build stability in an unstable world, something as solemn as rock. But it is also a dear thing—and the promise itself binds us together. Therefore, the signs of it are *unnecessary* but are treasures nevertheless: our golden rings; letters written in absence; certain anniversary traditions.

But there are husbands and wives for whom the promise itself is *not* enough. Their certainty, their personal stability in an unstable world, cannot be built on mere promises, since each sees the other as potentially a part *of* that unstable world! Therefore, they create legal signs to establish the promise. They bind one another to contracts constructed to outlast any promise of faithfulness: prenuptial agreements. These signs are not treasures. They are grim necessities made powerful by a codified judiciary.

Now, then, apply the same alternatives to our relationship with God. How do we react to the promises God makes unto us? In delight do we seek a keepsake?—or in doubt do we demand proofs?

Be wary, my friend: when God is the promisor, delight and doubt reveal no one but ourselves. For God is faithful. God is trustworthy (read Isa. 44:6–8). God is unlike the world altogether. He gives keepsakes of his promises, surely. Unto faith, God grants signs in abundance: rainbows, pillars of fire and cloud, water in the wilderness, lightning to consume Elijah's wet sacrifice, and this sign: "Behold, a virgin shall conceive and bear a son, and shall call his name Immanuel."

Again, God is faithful. He does not change. Therefore, if we feel that we must bind him to his promises by some sign, some extra proof (which for God is precisely as insulting as it is unnecessary), we will only bind ourselves. That sign will burden us like a punishment. And more than we ourselves shall suffer for this, *our* faithlessness.

∽

So the angel Gabriel has just announced that Zechariah and Elizabeth will have the son they prayed for. Moreover, the angel enriched his message with detail, giving them a name of their son, describing his life and his very purpose, declaring him to be the keeping of ancient promises *(God keeps promises!)*—and doing it all in song!

So what is old Zechariah thinking after heaven put on such a show?

He's thinking, "Can't be."

He's got his head stuck in this created world. The old realist can't see beyond creation to the Creator.

"What you say is wonderful and all," he says to the Messenger of Heaven, "but I'm too old for dreaming, too old for raising children. And even if I could, I'm married to a woman too old to bear them."

Now, if Zechariah were trusting the good news of the messenger, Gabriel's next words would fill him with immortal delight, for by them the old priest would realize that he is seeing the one who sees the face of God, a God trustworthy and true.

"I," cries the angel, "am Gabriel. I, who stand in the presence of God, am sent to give you this good news."

But Zechariah is *mis*trusting, *dis*believing. His question is meant literally: "How shall I know this? By what proof shall I know the truth of this news?"

I stand in the presence of God, in this case, sounds terrible, for it means: *God sends this news! It is God whom you mistrust!*

And the answer to Zechariah's question, the proof God gives that he does keep his promises, is no treasure. It binds the old man with a heavy burden hard to bear: "You will be mute until the day these things come to pass."

More than Zechariah suffers this "sign." All the worshipers outside do too, for the priest cannot utter over them the Aaronic blessing for which they have come. No one says, "The Lord bless you and keep you . . ."

Friend, unto you the Lord says, "Surely I am coming soon" (Rev. 22:20).

And what do you say to that promise? Do you by your unconscious behavior utter doubt? Does an earthbound vision deny the possibility? Are you scared to consider an end to the world?

"Can't be."

"Prove it."

Sadly, the sign of our mistrust shall be *the doubt itself*, together with all the anxieties and suspicions and loneliness which doubt engenders. And these will last until we come to trust, or else until his coming comes to pass.

Jesus says, "I am coming soon!"

And how do you respond? Oh, let it be as a bride responds to the promise of the bridegroom, adorning yourself for his return, joyfully shouting with the Spirit, "Come!" (Rev. 21:2, 9; 22:17). Then your joy, your present beauty, your complete sense of assurance and belonging—*these* shall be signs of the Lord's trustworthiness and of our trust, signs of his love until he comes in glory.

"Amen! Come, Lord Jesus!"

Almighty God:

Grant us, with your marvelous promises, a trust equally as marvelous, both in you and in the goodness to come.

Jesus:

Grant us, with this marvelous trust, a delight equally as marvelous, a joy to uphold our whole existence until the day when it comes to pass, indeed, that you come in glory among us.

Holy Spirit:

Grant us with this marvelous delight, a service equally as marvelous, so that all we do bespeaks our joy, our trust, and our God's great faithfulness!

Amen

Ah, Zechariah, You Who Doubted: *What a Model of Obedience You've Become*

LUKE 1:24–25:

> *After these days Zechariah's wife Elizabeth conceived, and for five months she kept herself in seclusion.*
> *"This is what the Lord has done for me," she said, "when he looked favorably on me and took away the disgrace I have endured among my people."*

FOR FIVE MONTHS there are only two who know: you, Zechariah, and your wife. Why is that? Why do you maintain such a silence regarding the miracle growing in Elizabeth's womb?

Well, yes: you cannot speak. That's true.

Neither can Elizabeth speak to you as she used to do (cf. Luke 1:62). She has to make signs to make sense. That limits the discourse between you.

So maybe the enormity of the event, as signified by this radical reduction of communication in your house, has persuaded the two of you to keep it a secret. Maybe you are more than dumb: dumb*founded* by the nearness of the Deity unto you.

Or have you already written down for her the prophecy that comes with this child? The Elijah-quality? That he, John, the baby for whom the two of you are now preparing, will himself prepare a whole people for the coming of the Lord? And if so, does the child already diminish the two of you in your own eyes? Are you somehow overshadowed by the divine selection of your son and *humbled* into quietude?

Actually, I would have thought you'd go running through the neighborhood with such elemental news.

True, true, you cannot talk—but Elizabeth can, and she has endured the reproaches of her whole community almost as long as the two of you have been married. Why wouldn't *she* rush to tell others the news that she's going to have a baby, after all? She *knows* that the Lord has "taken away my disgrace." She murmurs the phrase continually like the verse of a psalm, a sweet song of thanksgiving. And there is absolutely no custom that commands women to seclude themselves during the first months of pregnancy. No one does that. The news is too beautiful.

But maybe Elizabeth is a little fearful that the child won't come to term. Perhaps she's suppressing any desire to boast, since telling the news too soon would turn it into a mortal shame if something interrupted it. Like a miscarriage. What if the gossips who reproached her and who then were humbled by her pregnancy, next heard the sad retraction that there'd be no baby after all? Oh, how they would redouble the reproach! The end would be worse than the beginning.

Some people think it's unlucky to utter the precious thing at all. Naming it makes it known to good and evil alike, and since evil hates happiness, it will strive to destroy what makes you glad. Is that what you think?

Or maybe you were savoring it, keeping the child unto yourselves awhile before you had to give him away (as Hannah did Samuel) to God and to the whole world.

But your silence keeps many things a secret—even the motive for the silence itself. Whatever the reason, it is *your* reason alone, yours and Elizabeth's. We can never know it.

∞

But in the fact that you are able to keep more silences than one, Zechariah, I find a remarkable lesson regarding our relationship to the God whom we—you and I—serve in this world.

That you have been made mute by Gabriel may signify your doubt and the truth of God's promise. That was an act of God, surely.

But that you can *choose* for a full five months to keep secret the actual event signifies how real is your own participation in God's plans! Surely, this is *your* act. Yet it matches the Lord's. You are partners!

God is working *with* you to accomplish his desires for the world! Neither you nor Elizabeth is a mere puppet of the Deity. None of us is. After you returned from your duties in Jerusalem, in the night when you made wordless love with your wife so that God might love the world thereby, that was not the blind compulsion of sexual urges. Nor was it an act coerced by a controlling God. It was obedience! And true obedience was ever an act of freedom, never the reaction to oppression. Obedience unto God is personal participation in the love of God!

Even so let me willingly match my action to the will of the Lord. Whatever my immediate reasons for choosing to be like him, let the larger one ever be thanks that he chose to be like me, to save me from my sin.

Then blessed am I. And blessed are we all. Blessed is everyone through whom God reaches into this world to love others, for we are partners in the Gospel from this day until the day of Jesus, when God shall bring our good work to completion.

O Lord Jesus:

You have chosen me to serve you by serving your people here in the world. Such choosing proves your love for me and for the world.

Now I, my Lord, also choose. I pledge to serve you by serving your people here, in my world. Freely, joyfully I obey your word, because I love you more than anything.

Yes! Yes, I do.

PART THREE

Mary

DECEMBER SEVEN

An Exhortation:
Daily to Join the Sisterhood of Mary

LUKE 1:26–27:

> *In the sixth month the angel Gabriel was sent from God to a city of Galilee named Nazareth, to a virgin betrothed to a man of the House of David whose name was Joseph.*
>
> *The virgin's name was Mary.*

READ, TOO: MATTHEW 1:1–16,
  (ESPECIALLY VERSES 3, 5, 6, 16)

IN THE GREEK, this twenty-seventh verse is the only place in all Scripture where one might read that Mary is "of the house of David." In many places Joseph is clearly identified with the lineage of David. It's likelier that his wife was born a Levite, like her kinswoman Elizabeth.

Nevertheless, if not by blood and birth, then by grace and by *character* this woman joins the genealogy of the Messiah!

Hebrew genealogies almost never mentioned women. Yet Matthew names four in the ancestry of the Christ. Not one of them is here by birth. Each becomes a matriarch of Jesus, rather, by her character and by God's grace. This is the sisterhood that Mary is about to enter.

53

And these are models—both for Mary, who shall carry Jesus in her womb, and for us, who carry him in our hearts and our behavior.

∞

1. Christian, in a world both careless and unkind, be cunning and courageous (Gen. 38)!

When *Tamar* (a Canaanite) married Er, the eldest son of the patriarch Judah, she married sorrow. Er was evil and died young. By law, then, Tamar was required to bear a child by Judah's second son. But that fellow was no better than the first. He refused his duty. So Judah sent Tamar to her father's house, there to live as a widow until his third son grew up.

But she languished at her father's house. Judah forgot her. Tamar would have remained a widow forever, except that she became as "wise as a serpent, as innocent as the dove" (Matt. 10:16).

When one day she learned that Judah was traveling nearby, she put off her widow's weeds and veiled herself and sat where the man might see her. He saw her. He thought her a harlot, and bargained for her body.

"What do you want?" he said.

"As a pledge for your future payment," said she, "your signet ring, your cord, and the staff in your right hand."

Consider now the passion of mighty men—and the cunning of women who must remind them of righteousness: Judah gave her all these.

When Tamar became pregnant; when Judah learned that his daughter-in-law had offended the family by "playing the harlot"; when he commanded her to be burned, that bold woman appeared before him and said, "By the man to whom these belong, am I with child."

Oh, what a perilous game she played, now placing before Judah his own signet, his cord, and the staff of his right hand.

But he said, "She is more righteous than I."

∞

2. Christian, our second matriarch defines what we with Mary must become: "room," the real inn and lodging place for the Savior. For that's what *Rahab's* name means: "room" (Josh. 2).

Rahab was a citizen of Jericho. Yet when Joshua sent two men to spy inside the enemy walls, she chose against her culture, against her own world, and gave these men "room" of the highest kind, a safe place, protection for their lives. The king of Jericho sought to kill them. But this woman of Jericho hid them on the roof of her house, that they might lead Israel over Jordan into the Promised Land.

Even so Mary shall keep Jesus in her womb, her home, and her heart. And so may we keep him in our behavior, that he, Jesus, might lead the whole world over Jordan into the Promised Land.

∞

3. Ah, what gentle fidelity our third matriarch models!

Ruth was a Moabite. Nevertheless, to Bethlehem she traveled when her husband died, because she stayed faithful to her mother-in-law, Naomi. How obedient she was to the woman who called herself *bitterness*. How gracious to Naomi's kinsman, Boaz.

How beautiful the story of their love.

And how blessed Naomi, when she could finally shed bitterness and take up joy again; for a son was born to Ruth, the one who became the father of the father of David the King.

Likewise, Mary shall be both faithful and obedient to God, the Father of her son. And can we be any less? Of course not. Fidelity in us should likewise make a beautiful story.

4. Finally *Bath-sheba* joined the ancestry of the Messiah as Tamar and Ruth did, through suffering and loss (2 Sam. 11 and 12).

Bath-sheba, raped by the king who next killed her husband.

Bath-sheba, under the cruelty of men to grieve the death of her firstborn son.

Bath-sheba, who witnessed the change in David from strutting sinner, to downcast penitent, to the one anointed by God—for this is the power of forgiveness, even to transfigure the human heart.

Bath-sheba, torn between the meanness and the majesty of humankind, for her second son rose to rule the kingdom when his father David had died.

Bath-sheba: she signals the paradox for all who carry the Lord into the world. Mary shall find both cruelty and majesty in the crucifixion of her son. And we shall be torn, for Jesus' sake, between suffering and grace, since his name draws hatred, yet his is the forgiveness that transfigures the heart.

O Christian, then let this be your striving:

With three to make your heart bold and spacious and faithful; and with the fourth matriarch to learn forgiveness.

But with Mary, now, let this be your prayer:

That the Lord would enter you spiritually, as bodily he entered her; and that daily he might through you enter the world as once he was born from her.

Amen

A Call:
To Self-Examination, and to Fear!

LUKE 1:28–30:

> *And Gabriel came to Mary and addressed her thus:*
>
> *"Hail, O favored one, the Lord is with you!"*
>
> *Now, she was greatly troubled at what he said and wondered what such a greeting might mean.*
>
> *But the angel said to her, "Do not be afraid, Mary, for you have found favor with God."*

THIS, TOO, MUST absolutely be a part of our Christmas anticipations: that in the presence of divinity we are "greatly troubled."

When he saw the seraphim flying and heard their cries, the prophet Isaiah wailed, "Woe is me! I am lost, for I am a man of unclean lips!" (Isa. 6:1–5). Even the reflected glory of the Lord, flaming in the face of a living man, caused such mortal dread that the people of Israel "were afraid to come near" Moses after he had talked with the Lord (Ex. 34:30).

Nevertheless, fear has been much forgotten—both by the world and by Christians in general. We rush toward angels unafraid. We approach the blazing furnaces of the seraphim with no more apprehension than children who reach laughingly for fire.

This fearlessness is not a sign of the character of God, as if God has changed through the centuries that divide us from Moses and Isaiah, from Zechariah and Mary and the shepherds. Rather, it is a sign of the character of this present age, of arrogance or of ignorance, whether or not one admits to a living God.

Mindlessly do the bells of secular celebrations jingle for Christmas. Meaninglessly do carols repeat their tinny joys in all the malls in America. No richer than soda pop is every sentimentalized Christmas special on TV. Fearless is the world at play with godly things, because Godless is its heart.

If God is a laughing Santy, why should we be afraid?

Secular arrogance says there is no God. Arrogance, in fact, assumes that humanity itself—its dreams, its talents, its visions and accomplishments—is the nearest thing to God the world will ever know. Therefore, the "true meaning of Christmas" is assumed to be the occasional human kindness which, yes, may very well be symbolized by a nice old gentleman.

Or secular ignorance takes creation for its Creator; it worships the earth, the universe, the great cosmos both material and immaterial. It believes that goodness itself is God. So it finds divinity in good little children. And its Christmas celebrates not the birth of God among us, but birth *itself*: that humans do renew themselves, starting fresh in infant faces, returning to innocence. Of course the secular angel is a chubby babe with vestigial wings.

How can there be fear in such a Christmas? No God. No blinding righteousness approaching the earth. No gulf between us and the immortal Invisible—and so, no need to bridge the gulf.

⚭

Surely we Christians should know better. Yet look around: are we more fearful at the prospect of angels than the world is? Aren't we blithe this Christmas too? Heedless? Jaunty, even, to the point of self-satisfaction?

Of course it is right to rejoice in tidings of great joy: that the mercy of God now crosses the gulf which our sinning opened between ourselves and our Creator. Yes, it is right to fall down in perfect trust, fearlessly, before the Christ child and to worship him. Yes, it is right to delight in the song of the angels, the peace that God brings to the earth. Yes, yes, and therefore do we cry in confidence, "Fear not! Fear not! For God hath banished fear!"

Ah, friend, but arrogance assumes that we *deserve* this blessed state. There is neither grace nor gifts for those who deserve what they get—and no true joy at the receiving.

And ignorance forgets the sin without which mercy means nothing, without which the baby Jesus is just a baby after all.

Listen: the light of Christmas shines *into darkness!* We should be the walking dead. What we deserve, in fact, is the absence of God—a cold and cosmic isolation—for this is our sin, that we chose to be gods in the place of God. In the day we disobeyed we began to die. We should, therefore, be dwelling in a land of deep darkness, mistrust, hatreds, hopelessness, finality, and death.

But here in a child comes God, the light! And light in darkness is a frightening thing. ("People loved darkness rather than light, because their deeds were evil" John 3:19.)

O my friend, a self-examination both humble and true must cause us to tremble before the living God. Yes!—we will be "greatly troubled" at the appearing of angels.

But even as we feared, so do we rejoice when we hear the light say, "Don't be afraid. I have not come to punish but to give you life. I am no judge. I am the Savior born for you."

Life instead of death? That is a wonder! And the wonder is all the more intense because death had been expected—because death had been right!

The mercy of God? Is not this a dazzling wonder?

And isn't Christmas wonderful after all?

O Jesus Christ,

Rule my heart in truth and grace, and make my gladness prove the glories of your righteousness and wonders of your love, and wonders of your love.

Amen

A Teaching:
What Sort of King Will the Son of David Be?

LUKE 1:31–33:

> *The angel said to Mary:*
> *"And behold, you will conceive in your womb and bear a son, and you will call his name Jesus. He will be great. He will be called the Son of the Most High. The Lord God will give him the throne of his father David. He will reign over the house of Jacob for ever, and of his kingdom there will be no end."*

So NOW, THE WORD. The very first word of the herald from heaven, announcing the child to come.

Who is he? What sort of hero approaches? What *is* this Mercy soon to be born among us?

Why, he shall be a king! He shall be *the* king whom God had promised a thousand years earlier to David—not only a king *like* David, but a king to fulfil all that David represented. For David was a king bounded by time and space. His reign existed within the history of humankind. But this King shall gather time and space into his kingdom, and shall himself embrace the history of humankind, for of his kingdom "there will be no end."

David was anointed a son of God. David was adopted: "He said to me, 'You are my son, today I have begotten you'"(Psalm 2:7). But this one will be *born* "Son of the Most High."

Read the dialogue that the first King David had with God in 2 Samuel 7:8–16. After he had built himself a house of cedar, David desired to build a house for the dwelling of the Lord. But God denied him that desire. What even the best of humans could produce was too confining for God. It never was what we could accomplish that established a lasting relationship with God, but what God himself promises to accomplish for us. Therefore, to the golden king, that most glorious ruler of the Old Testament, God promised a New Testament.

David said, "I want to make you a house."

And God responded with heavenly hilarity, a pun: "No, but I will make *you* a house"(v. 11). David was himself to *become* a lasting household, for the Lord said, "When you lie down with your fathers, I will raise up your offspring after you … and I will establish his kingdom. He shall build a house for my name, and I will establish the throne of his kingdom for ever. I will be his father, and he shall be my son."

In the short view, God was looking at the physical child of David, Solomon.

But in the eternal view, God was looking at the son of Mary, the only begotten "Son of the Most High." And here is the deeper meaning of the angel's words: Messiah is coming. In Messiah shall the house of God be built (wherein, with God, we all may dwell eternally). In Messiah shall goodness finally arise to rule the world. In Messiah shall we find a place of peace; for "I will appoint a place for my people Israel," said the Lord (v. 10). "I will plant them that they may dwell in their own place and be disturbed no more. Violent people shall afflict them no more . . . and I will give you rest from all your enemies."

This is he who is to come; this is the hero: Jesus.

"You shall call his name Jesus."

Jesus. He is our mercy. Jesus. Jesus.

Jesus:

> *Name of wondrous love, name all other*
> *names above,*
> *Unto which must every knee bow in deep humility.*

Jesus:

> *Name decreed of old to the maiden mother told—*
> *Kneeling in her lowly cell—by the angel Gabriel.*

Jesus:

> *Name of priceless worth to the children*
> *of the earth*
> *For the promise that it gave, "Jesus shall his*
> *people save."*

Jesus:

> *Name of wondrous love, human name of*
> *God above;*
> *Pleading only this, we flee, helpless, O our God,*
> *to Thee.*

Amen

(Words by William W. How, 19th century)

A Teaching:
What Sort of Child Is Born of Holiness and Humanity?

LUKE 1:34–37:

> *Mary said to the angel, "How can this be, since I've never had relations with a man?"*
>
> *The angel answered, "The Holy Spirit will come upon you, and power from the Most High will overshadow you. So the child to be born will be called holy—Son of God."*
>
> *And the angel said, "Behold, your kinswoman Elizabeth has in spite of her old age conceived a son. Yes, and this is already the sixth month for a woman who was said to be barren. For with God nothing will be impossible."*

A REASONABLE HUMAN QUESTION receives an answer that exceeds all human reason. It exceeds, too, the natural law. But the angel turns from rules to the Ruler. He grounds the truth of his answer not in creation but in the Creator, whose word shall never be impossible.

By the promise of God an old and barren woman conceives. But that diminishes next to this, that by the promise of God a *virgin* shall as well conceive.

Born of the barren woman, John is less than him who shall be born of the virgin, for John prepares the way, but Jesus *is* the Way. John's parents both are human.

But the father of Jesus is God.

And that precisely is the substance of Gabriel's answer to Mary.

She says, "This is the way of all flesh."

And Gabriel answers, *But you are about to see the ways of God.*

Mary says, "No baby was ever conceived without a man as father."

And Gabriel answers, *This baby's father shall be no man. His father shall be God.*

Mary says, "In every child the characteristics of both parents are manifest together."

And Gabriel agrees: *Yes, Jesus will be flesh like you—and like God he will be holy, truly the Son of God.*

And that is the meaning of this brief exchange between Mary's most human question and the angel's godly response: that Jesus is both! He is human, as fully human as his mother; and he is at the same time as divine as his Father, the Most High.

From this grand paradox flows the whole of our Christian faith. Without it our truth is human only; or else Truth is hidden in the heavenly regions, unknowable by us.

And a Christmas reduced to anything less than this is no Christmas at all—this, this paradox: that the Word (which was in the beginning with God, and *was* God) became flesh and dwelt among us full of grace and truth (John 1:1–14).

Of the Father's love begotten, ere the worlds
*   began to be,*
He is alpha and omega, he the source,
*   the ending he,*
Of the things that are, that have been, and that
*   future years shall see*
*   Evermore and evermore.*

Oh, that birth forever blessed when the virgin,
*   full of grace,*
By the Holy Ghost conceiving, bare the Savior
*   of our race,*
And the babe, the world's Redeemer,
*   first revealed his sacred face*
*   Evermore and evermore.*

O ye heights of heaven, adore him; angel hosts,
*   his praises sing;*
Powers, dominions, bow before him and extol
*   our God and King.*
Let no tongue on earth be silent, every voice
*   in concert ring*
*   Evermore and evermore.*

Christ, to thee with God the Father and,
*   O Holy Ghost, to thee*
Hymn and chant and high thanksgiving and
*   unending praises be,*
Honor, glory, and dominion, and eternal victory
*   Evermore and evermore.*

Amen

(*Corde natus ex Parentis*, Aurelius C. Prudentius, 4th century;
translators, John M. Neale and Henry W. Baker, 19th century)

O Mary:
How Blessed Is Your "Yes!"

LUKE 1:38:

> *Mary answered the angel, "Behold, I am the maid-servant of the Lord. Let it happen to me according to your word."*
>
> *And the angel departed from her.*

MARY, MOTHER OF our Lord, I wish I could be as pure a disciple as you were even from the beginning!

For you were invited to join a sisterhood—with Tamar and Bath-sheba—of sorrow and human suffering, since the child of your womb would draw the hatreds and the outrages of a scoundrel world.

And you said, "Yes."

For you were asked to serve faithfully on behalf of others, like Rahab to protect a few for the sake of the many, like Ruth to turn disappointment into joy.

And you said, "Yes."

For it was an angel that spoke to you, a sky-strider, an inhabitant of holy heaven whose face caught fire from standing near to God, whose glory darkened all the common world in which you lived.

Yet you did not hesitate in fear or horror. You said, "Yes."

For history was pouring into your womb, the whole history of the Israel backward through David even unto Abraham; yet you were but a single person, one lone woman. How could a vessel of simple human limitation hold twenty centuries of national endeavor—triumph, failure, sin, atonement, trouble, prayer, and promise—and *not* burst open? But you *would* burst, Mary. You would spew the son of David into Judah again, and he would keep every past promise of God.

And you said, "Yes."

For heaven itself was swelling within you, and you were the door. Not in terrible glory would he come, this Son of the Most High God. Not in the primal blinding light, nor as the shout by which God uttered the universe, nor yet with the trumpet that shall conclude it, but through your human womb, as an infant bawling and hungry. By your labor, Mary, by the fierce contractions of your uterus, eternity would enter time. The angel said, *Will you be the door of the Lord into this place?*

And you said, "Yes."

Two thousand years before you, another woman heard an angel declare that she would bear a son. Sarah was very old then. Ninety years old. And because of her great age, she laughed. Her reaction to the impossible promise was a disbelieving, scornful snort: "After I'm old and my husband is old, shall I have pleasure?" To her the angel said what Gabriel said to you: *Is anything too hard for the Lord?* (Gen. 18:9–15; see also Job 42:2 and Matt. 19:26).

Ah, Mary, but your reaction to a promise more impossible than Sarah's was a sweet, complete obedience and faith: "Let it happen to me according to your word."

You, the first of all the disciples of Jesus, said, "Yes."

Heavenly Father:

Thank you for the faith of a maiden, in whose obedience your plan for the reconciliation of the whole world was begun.

I beg you, too, that you might empower me in pure simplicity. Teach my mouth and all my parts to make this single response to whatever task you set before me—this:

Let it be to me according to your word.
"Yes!"

Amen

PART FOUR

Elizabeth

DECEMBER TWELVE

The Story:
Two Mothers Meet

LUKE 1:39–41A:

> *In those days Mary arose and went hastily into the hill country to a Judean city. There she entered the house of Zechariah and greeted Elizabeth. And when Elizabeth heard Mary's greeting, the baby jumped in her womb.*

LAUGH, ELIZABETH! Laugh with excitement. Something's coming. Something's happening. Like springtime in winter, it's not just you who's pregnant. The infant within you—he's not the only thing about to burst new into creation.

Behold, says the Lord, *I am doing a new thing; now it springs forth: do you not perceive it?* (Isa. 43:19).

For whatever reason (we don't know the reason) old Elizabeth has kept her condition a secret all these months. Who else knows that she is pregnant? Zechariah. Her husband, who goes about his business in a mute, grinning hilarity. But he can keep a secret.

So no one else knows about it!

73

Yet all at once Elizabeth is peering in a mirror, for here is someone who knows what she knows. She's peering in a rich, three-dimensioned mirror, for here is the body of one who's experiencing what she is experiencing. And the mirror she peers in, why, it is also a window! For it opens up on a wonderful vista, broader than two women and two pregnancies put together!

⤫

Elizabeth is dozing on the roof of her house. It has become her habit to take brief midday naps because her old bones are unused to the weight of the baby and the plain labor it adds to her every waking motion.

Suddenly, as if the air itself has rung, she snaps awake, all her senses trembling. She can hear footsteps, small and swift and far away. Someone is running on tiptoe. Elizabeth feels a pressure on her chest, as if the weather were changing toward storm—yet she can, it seems to her, taste the very radiance of the sun. Something's happening! Someone's coming!

Elizabeth lifts herself and looks over the parapet of the roof. Yes! Yes, a woman is running the hills in her direction. Very intent. Filled with purpose and a certain knowledge. *Who?*—

Immediately Elizabeth knows who! She can't see the features, but she recognizes the posture and the gestures, the bold pitching of her arms in time with her feet: it's her kinswoman. Mary. *But why?*—

The old woman stands up and arranges her robes. She descends the ladder on the far side of the house into her courtyard. It doesn't take but a second, yet the instant her foot touches ground, there is Mary, as big as life, entering the doorway, beaming!

Elizabeth gasps. She can't breathe. Mary's bright eye (*something's strange!*) is piercing Elizabeth even to the secret in her soul. Mary knows! Here is the mirror of her mind. They've told no one, no one—yet this eager young woman knows that she, in spite of her old age, has conceived a baby in her womb and is pregnant. (*Who told her? What's happening?*)

Mary blooms. Like an opening rose, her whole being unfolds before Elizabeth, and in greeting she utters her kinswoman's name. She whispers, "Elizabeth!"

And straightway Elizabeth, too, flushes with a bright, pink joy and recognition. The sound of Mary's voice is so familiar! It sends forth news even as blossoms release their scent upon the wind: Mary, too, is pregnant! (*Something's happening!*) Elizabeth is on the edge of tears, for here in young, fresh Mary is the mirror of her own condition: sisters, sisters! They are both with child!

But before the tears drop; before the woman can rush her cousin to hug her; before she can utter the first word of greeting in return, the tiny prophet low in her womb expresses his first prophecy! Already filled with the Holy Spirit, already preparing the way, the baby leaps for joy at the sound of the voice of the mother of his Lord!

Oh, yes, something wonderful is happening! A new thing is springing forth into the world. All at once Elizabeth knows what it is, for she sees through the window of her cousin's condition into the mind of God: this is the Messiah!

And old Elizabeth can scarcely stand the excitement:

"Who am I?" she cries with a loud voice. "Who am I, that the mother of my Lord should come to me?"

∞

And so it begins. Now more than one is aware of the Advent stirring in the world: there are two who know. And each confirms the glad anticipation of the other. Two is a communion. Two is necessary. Two is a perfect circle: one to speak it, one to hear. The word is real. Christ is coming!

Christmas is coming!

    Christmas is coming. O Lord, my heart is hammering, my chest grows taut with excitement: you are coming! How can I help but laugh?

    Dear Lord, then send me one other, one blessed other person with whom to share my joy, one to hear me utter my faith in you, one to speak faith in return.

Christmas is coming!

Amen

Elizabeth's Blessing:
Makes Mary a Model for the Faithful

LUKE 1:41B–45

> *Elizabeth, filled with the Holy Spirit, proclaimed with a loud cry:*
> *"Blessed are you among women, and blessed is the fruit of your womb. Who am I that the mother of my Lord should come to me? For behold, the moment your greeting sounded in my ears, the baby in my womb jumped with gladness. Oh, how fortunate is she who believed that the Lord's words to her would be fulfilled!"*

Now ELIZABETH CRIES BLESSINGS upon Mary; and because the Holy Spirit is the source of her word, that word is both true and deep in its truth. It reveals much about the mother of Jesus.

Moreover, it sets Mary up as a model for us, that we might know both the cause of her blessedness, and its quality.

Come: with Mary join the family of Jesus—

1. Elizabeth points out the defining characteristic in Mary, the *personal cause* of her good fortune: "Fortunate (blessed!) is she who believed that the Lord's words to her would be fulfilled."

This is precisely what happened in the exchange between Mary and the messenger of the Lord: "The power of the Most High will overshadow you; therefore the child to be born will be called holy, the Son of God."

And to this promise of a miraculous birth, Mary brought the faith that engenders obedience. She believed the Lord's words, saying: "Let it happen to me according to your word."

Quickly, my friend, turn to Luke 11:27–28 where Jesus himself declares what made Mary most fortunate. An anonymous woman cries out that it must be Mary's physical motherhood: "How fortunate is the womb that bore you and the breasts you sucked!"

But Jesus revises the reasons for good fortune—and in the process he invites you and me as well to become kin to him as closely as his mother was kin: "No! Rather, fortunate are those who hear the word of God and keep it."

That's Mary! She receives the word of God in faith, and faith in her becomes obedience. *That*, is the cause of the good fortune which Elizabeth immediately recognizes.

Again, friend, turn quickly to Luke 8:19–21 in order to hear this invitation into the family of Jesus yet more clearly. When someone tells Jesus that his "mother and brothers are waiting outside," Jesus replies with the real cause of kinship: Who are his mother and his brothers? "Those who hear the word of God and do it."

Yep, that's Mary. And this particular means for joining the family of Jesus is one we all might share.

∞

2. Elizabeth's blessing of Mary reveals truths below the touchable surface of mere fact. In the Spirit she utters as well

the *quality* of Mary's blessed state—again, one which all who hear and keep the word of God might share.

In order to find the first model of Elizabeth's exclamation, turn to Deuteronomy 28. Moses is standing on the banks of the Jordan River. The children of Israel are just about to cross over, into the land that God had promised them. Moses will not go with them, but his blessings will—so long as "You," O Israel, "obey the voice of the Lord your God, being careful to do all his commandments which I command you this day."

Look closely at verse 4: "Blessed shall be the fruit of your body. . . ."

It is not accidental that this blessing is repeated by Elizabeth to Mary: *Blessed is the fruit of your womb.*

Now, then, read the expanded blessing which Moses grants to those who obey, to Israel at the edge of the fulfillment of God's promise, and to us at the edge of the coming of Christ, the edge of Christmas. "All these blessings shall come upon you, if you obey: Blessed in the city; blessed in the field; blessed the fruit of your body and of your ground, the fruit of your beasts, the increase of your cattle, the young of your flock; blessed the basket and your kneading trough—and you yourself, when you come in and when you go out."

God shall be our God, and God our providence. That is the quality of the blessing: a Christmas of abundant giving, equal not to our selfish desiring, but to our need.

3. But in this next Old Testament source for Elizabeth's blessing of Mary, Mary is discovered to stand alone: this one is hers uniquely, though we all take the benefit.

Turn to Judges 5:24ff. Deborah—a woman like Elizabeth singing in the Spirit of the Lord—utters blessing upon Jael in a form which the Spirit chooses for Mary.

Elizabeth: "Blessed are you *among women*."

Deborah: "Blessed *among women* be Jael."

Why? What has Jael done? She, one humble woman acting alone, struck the commander of the Canaanite forces, struck the leader of the enemies of the people of God, with a killing blow.

Likewise, Mary alone bore Christ into the world. This humble woman brought forth our Savior, who would himself strike down the forces that desire our defeat, sin and death and the devil!

So perish all thine enemies O Lord!

But thy friends be like the sun as he rises in his might!

Mary may be like Jael. She may stand for Israel and for all the family of Jesus, too.

But Elizabeth is Moses and Deborah, mighty voices of God.

O Lord:

What a wondrous weave your word creates throughout the history of your people! Certain themes keep reappearing, till finally I learn the richness of your love.

So the Christmas story regathers the words you've spoken before. And this Christmas repeats all the Christmases I've ever celebrated. Slowly, slowly I'm learning.

Amen

An Effusion:
What Singing at the Advent of Our King!

LUKE 1:46–49:

And Mary said:

"My soul magnifies the Lord,
And my spirit rejoices in God my Savior,
for he has regarded the low estate of
his handmaiden.
For behold, henceforth all generations will
call me blessed;
for he who is mighty has done great things for me,
and holy is his name."

THEY'RE SINGING SONGS in Palestine! They can't help it: canticles rise to their lips and to the ears of God spontaneously.

Gabriel twice has sung his sacred messages. Elizabeth made a loud and rhythmic cry of her blessings. Now Mary breaks into song: "My soul magnifies the Lord!"

And that's only the beginning.

Soon the mute Zechariah will do more than utter prosaic sentences; he'll sing a *Benedictus* at the birth of his son, the prophet of the Most High.

Then Gabriel will return to chant good news to the shepherds, and straightway he'll be joined by the whirling hosts of heaven, the angels of God in thunderous chorus: *Gloria in Excelsis!*

And still the people of Palestine sing—in older broken tones: for Simeon has a closing hymn, the *Nunc Dimittis* of his personal departure.

Altogether they create a thrilling exchange between heaven and earth. Oh!—I wish I could hear the antiphony. Gabriel and all the angels descending; earthbound throats whose songs ascend to heaven, worshipers not *recalling* some wonderful moment, but living the moment, knowing the moment, responding in the extremes of human awareness and art and high articulation.

O Lord, you are the musician, and we are all your instruments. You breathe, and we come to life. You breathe, and we are horns for your glory. You blow through the world the winds of the spirit, and we like chimes cannot keep silent. You pluck the strings of our hearts, and we become a psalm.

You come, and we must sing.

And now your Son is entering here, our dirty sphere, voiding himself of power to be born in human form. The hand of heaven is touching people as it never has before! Mary can't help it. The cause of song is in her womb. She is transfigured. And if the woman had been born with the voice of a frog, it doesn't matter: she is God's minstrel now.

> *My soul magnifies the Lord,*
> *And my spirit rejoices in God my Savior,*
> *for he has regarded the low estate of his handmaiden ...*
> *Holy is his name!*

We will sing carols again this Christmas.

Fill them, O Jesus!
Fill our hearts with your love.
Fill our songs with your windy Spirit.
Let nothing we sing be empty or noxious or
*   foolish or false.*
For if you will be the cause of our carols,
then we will have joined the heavenly choirs.
We, with Mary, may be transported,
and joy will shed joy on everyone.

Amen

Mary's Song:
Echoing the Songs of Prophets and Angels

LUKE 1:46–56

And Mary said:

"My soul magnifies the Lord,
And my spirit rejoices in God my Savior,

for he has regarded the low estate of
his handmaiden.
For behold, henceforth all generations will
call me blessed;
for he who is mighty has done great things for me,
and holy is his name.
His mercy is from generation to generation
on those who fear him.

He has shown strength with his arm.
He has scattered the proud in the imagination
of their hearts.
He has put down the mighty from their thrones
and exalted those of low degree.
He has filled the hungry with good things,
and sent the rich empty away.

He has helped his servant Israel
in the remembrance of his mercy,

> *as he spoke to our fathers,*
> *to Abraham and to his posterity for ever."*

And Mary remained with Elizabeth about three months, then returned home.

Iᴛ ʜᴀꜱ ʙᴇɢᴜɴ: the song that the prophet Habakkuk sang centuries ago it being fulfilled!

Habakkuk's hymn ends:

> *Yet I will rejoice in the Lord!*
>   *I will joy in the God of my salvation!*
> *God, the Lord, is my strength;*
>   *he makes my feet like hinds' feet;*
>   *he makes me walk on my high places!*

Mary's words "God, my Savior" are the same in Greek as Habakkuk's, "God of my salvation."

From two sides of the promises of God, a man and a woman sing duet. He has heard the promise-word, and believes it. She's been told of promise-keeping, and believes it. Salvation is surely coming to the people of God, and time itself collapses, all chronology contracts into that single fierce and burning moment when God acts among us.

But even as she sings across the times a duet with the prophet of old, Mary is singing across the *worlds* a duet with another figure altogether.

What, when God communicates a blessed message, is the first best thing to do with it? Why, *tell* it.

And how shall your joy affect the telling? How shall faith and gladness send the message straight to the hearts of your hearers? O Christian, *sing* it with highest delight!

Listen with remembering ears to the song that Mary sings, and you will find that Gabriel's message has swiftly been given a human voice (both for Elizabeth and for "all generations" thereafter). It never is just the intellectual *meaning* of the words that captures the messages of the Almighty! The messages consist as well of things that must be felt, *experienced*: God's ineffable love, our emotional and spiritual responses, elements whose truth cannot be objectively analyzed nor reduced to doctrine.

Praise and thanksgiving require more than our brains. They want our laughter, our capering bodies, our trembling delight, smiles and the sweet flush of delight—and song. Praise must be sung.

So Mary sings a duet with the angel, a celestial song that transcends all worlds, for the flaming servants of God do join our grateful, faithful choirs:

The power of the Most High will overshadow you, sang Gabriel, and Mary refrains that word "power" in the word "mighty": *He who is mighty has done great things for me*.

Of the child to be born, Gabriel sang, *He will be great*, and Mary echoes the word: *Great things for me!*

Well, and we know what great things, don't we? We ought to. We, too, are recipients.

In her life and in her child—and already now in her song—they become great things for "*all* who fear him." Her praise is generous. What is being done for Mary personally will embrace the faithful generally.

And as Gabriel sang: *Therefore, the child to be born will be called holy—Son of God*, so Mary sings: *And holy is his name!*

And as Gabriel sang: *Of his kingdom there will be no end*, so Mary sings the same endlessness—again, embracing the many: *His mercy is on those who fear him from generation to generation.*

So Mary sings with the prophet of old to show what promises God is keeping in her present.

And Mary sings with the angel of heaven to show how the events of her present shall embrace all future generations.

We are that future. We are embraced.

But who are we?

The proud look down on others because they do not look up to God.

We are, apart from God, those of low degree. We must be the hungry and the poor. It cannot be otherwise! No, it can't—or we would never, when God exalts us after all, sing as Mary sang: spontaneous praises and thanksgivings.

> *Now praise we Christ, the holy one,*
> *The blessed virgin Mary's son,*
> *Far as the glorious sun doth shine*
> *E'en to the world's remote confine.*
>
> *All honor unto Christ be paid,*
> *Pure offspring of the favored maid,*
> *With Father and with Holy Ghost,*
> *Till time in endless time be lost.*

(*Coelius Sedulius*, c. 450; German version, Luther, 1524)

A Teaching:
How Mercy Comes, What Mercy Is

LUKE 1:57–63

> *Now the time came for Elizabeth to give birth, and she bore a son. When her neighbors and relatives heard that the Lord had shown great mercy to her, they rejoiced together with her.*
>
> *On the eighth day they gathered to circumcise the child, and they were going to name him Zechariah after his father.*
>
> *But his mother said, "Oh, no you don't! He's to be called John."*
>
> *They argued with her: "No one in your family has that name." And they made signs to his father, asking what he wanted the child to be called.*
>
> *Zechariah asked for a writing tablet, then astonished everyone by writing:* His name is John.

ELIZABETH, HOW DIFFICULT was it for an old woman to bring an infant to term? You did it almost alone. No one knew but your husband and your cousin Mary.

And the midwife: when mute Zechariah went and brought her to your house, and she entered your room and saw your condition, how astonished was she?

With what sort of grin did you greet her? And how quickly did the grin twist into a grimace when that mighty muscle contracted to drive a baby into the world?

O mother Elizabeth, how did it feel to bear a baby in your old age?

∞

The Lord has shown great mercy to you.

Literally, the word is: "The Lord *magnified* his mercy with you." It's the same word that Mary used in her hymn of praise.

And this *great mercy* shown to you, Elizabeth, is exactly what Mary meant when she sang: "His mercy is on those who fear him." You fear him.

You are one of low degree whom God your Savior has exalted. You are the hungry whom he will fill with good things.

And this is how "Mercy" always comes to us, isn't it?— like a baby delivered in old age: the miracle we thought we had outlived, the gift we thought impossible to receive. It always astonishes us.

And this is how "Mercy" comes—like a baby: something which, *through* us, God gives *to* us; something completely new and whole on its own; the gift we ourselves must serve and nourish; the gift, nevertheless, that grows up and loves us and finally carries us when we tremble in our dotage.

And this is what "Mercy" is: that which fulfills our heart's desire, that which gives purpose to our lives, that which also allows us not only to be loved, but also to love completely.

So God grants you this child, and that is his mercy.

So when God grants me the healing I could not expect (whether of my body or my spirit—or of the bodies and spirits of those I love) that is his mercy to me.

So when peace comes into me, though I had been desperately restless and afraid; and when I, who am weak, act with surprising strength; and when faith arises in my hopeless soul; and when I, whose heart was filled with hatreds, suddenly find forgiveness there; and when others love me, though I know I could not be the source of their loving; and when my children come home with reverence; and when the work of my hand praises God beyond my natural skill; and when what I am is what I ought to be—when*ever* the impossible gift arrives for me, it is God. It is evidence of his love. It is his mercy so great, that those around me (my neighbors and relatives) are astonished to find me in such a blessed condition after all.

Then let no one call the gift by some earthly name. Though it is I who now must nourish the gift (peace, forgiveness, faith), let no worldly voice argue that I am the source, that I earned or deserve it.

The gift that developed within me was not passed down from my parentage to me, not from my race, my culture, my education, prestige, or position. Nor could it arise from my own self, my nature or my doing.

This great mercy must receive the name God gives to it: John. *Johanan: The Lord has been gracious.*

∞

God bless you, Mother Elizabeth! Your experience trains me in my own. Your Christmas present teaches me how to receive mine. You have become a midwife to me.

Elizabeth, you bore the son
Who went before the holy one;
But it was you who went before
   The mother of our Lord.

'Twas you your cousin watched to see
How she might bear her own baby;
So I watch you, the one who bore
   The mercy of the Lord.

                      Amen

PART FIVE

John

A Teaching:
What John Becomes for Every Advent

LUKE 1:63–66

> *Zechariah asked for a writing tablet, then aston-ished everyone be writing*, His name is John. *Imme-diately his mouth was opened, his tongue loosed, and he began to utter praises to God.*
>
> *Fear fell on their neighbors. These events were dis-cussed throughout the whole hill country of Judea, and all who heard them stored them in their hearts, won-dering,* "What will this child become, then?"—*for the hand of the Lord was with him. . . .*
>
> *As the child grew up, he became strong in the spirit, and he stayed in the wilderness until the day of his public appearance in Israel.*

HERE, IN LUKE'S TELLING, are five marvelous and fearful events that surrounded the birth of John, evidence that the Lord was up to something:

—She who conceived him and bore him was very old.

—At his circumcision, his mother chose an odd name, and though the father was deaf to it, he wrote in clay the self-same name. What a tremendous, mysterious harmony between these two!

—But that harmony came straight from God, since their common act was the first fulfillment of Gabriel's prophecy to Zechariah: *You shall call his name John*.

—The second angelic prophecy had already been fulfilled, for there *were* "many rejoicing at his birth"(compare vv. 14 and 58).

—And the third prophecy was fulfilled the instant Zechariah wrote *John*. Though friends and relatives could not have realized that Zechariah's action was directly connected to heaven, the action itself was marvelous enough to astonish them. For suddenly the man who had been mute nine months erupted voluble praises to God.

No, this was no common birth. Yes, the hand of the Lord was clearly with this infant. What, then, would the Lord require of him hereafter? What was his function in the plans of God?

What, the people wondered, will this child become?

By this question and by that concluding reference to the child's life "in the wilderness until the day of his public appearance," Luke's story forces us to contemplate what the child in fact became: John the Baptist, "The voice of one crying in the wilderness, 'Prepare the way of the Lord!' "

Christian, that advent of Jesus two thousand years ago is not the actual Advent yet to come for us.

As John, who cried *Prepare* to Israel, was the messenger of that first appearing, so John is the messenger now of the reappearing, the Second Coming of Christ!

Still, still he cries: *Prepare!*

Are we listening?

Do we, who are busy preparing for Christmas, parties and presents and decorations and food and church programs—and visitors—do we prepare with equal fervor for the visitation of the Lord?

What sort of Advent *is* this imminent Advent for you? If you are consumed by one more Christmas (one mere Christmas among two thousand) your Advent is fleeting, time-bound, and likely self-absorbed. Desperate preparations often indicate an anxiety about the opinions of others regarding ourselves. But if your participation in this temporal Advent truly signifies preparations for the final Advent, you are Christ-absorbed.

An anonymous poem, written when there were still kings in the land, expresses the failure to read the marvelous and fearful signs that surround the holy birth:

> *Yet, if His Majesty, our sovereign Lord,*
> *Should of his own accord*
> *Friendly himself invite*
> *And say, "I'll be your guest tomorrow night"—*
> *How should we stir ourselves, call and command*
> *All hands to work: "Let no man idle stand;*
>
> *Set me fine Spanish tables in the hall;*
> *See they be fitted all,*
> *That there be room to eat*
> *And order taken that there want no meat;*
> *See every sconce and candlestick made bright*
> *That without tapers they may give a light;*
>
> *Look to the presents; are the carpets spread?*
> *The daisy o'er the head?*
> *The cushions in the chairs?*
> *And all the candles lighted on the stairs?*
> *Perfume the chambers and in any case*
> *Let each man give attendance in this place."*

Thus, if a king were coming, would we do;
And 'twere good reason, too,
For 'tis a duteous thing
To show all honor to our earthly king;
And after all our travail and our cost
So he be pleased to think no labor lost.

But at the coming of the King of Heaven
All's set at six and seven;
We wallow in our sin;
Christ cannot find a chamber in the inn.
We entertain him always like a stranger,
And, as at first, still lodge him in a manger.

Christ, awaken us to your coming again—and
give us the broom for making us clean!

Amen

An Exhortation:
Serve as Zechariah Defines Service

LUKE 1:67–79

*And Zechariah his father was filled with the Holy
Spirit, so that he prophesied, saying:*

"Blessed be the Lord God of Israel:

*for he has visited and redeemed his people,
and has raised up for us a horn of salvation
in the house of his servant David,
as he spoke by the mouth of his holy prophets
    from of old,
that we should be saved from our enemies,
and from the hand of all who hate us;
performing the mercy promised to our fathers,
and remembering his holy covenant,
the oath he swore to our father Abraham,
to grant that we, being delivered from the hand
    of our enemies,
might serve him without fear,
in holiness and righteousness before him all
    the days of our lives.*

*And you, child, will be called the prophet of the
    Most High;
for you will go before the Lord to prepare
    his ways,*

to give knowledge of salvation to his people
in the forgiveness of their sins,
through the tender mercy of our God,
when the day shall dawn upon us from on high
to give light to those who sit in darkness and
in the shadow of death,
to guide our feet into the way of peace."

GIVE US THE BROOM *for making us clean*.

With that abrupt prayer we ended our meditations yesterday—since perhaps we had noticed in our Christmas preparations a lack of readiness for the reappearing of Jesus "in his glory, all the angels with him, when he will sit on his glorious throne" (Matt. 25:31).

We pray first to learn what we ought to be to meet our King.

And second we pray to learn how we might become it.

And lo: Zechariah's song—turning our attentions again to John the Baptist—answers both our beggings.

∽

What, then, shall we be?

Servants, as Mary was, surely: so completely committed to this sacred service that it becomes our life's purpose; it shapes all our behavior; it defines, then, even our personhood. "This," said Mary, "is who I am. This is my identity. I am the handmaid of the Lord." Her body and soul together were given unto God, for God's word *dwelt* in her not only as an infant, but more especially as the very substance of her obedience. In this latter way may the word of God take flesh and breath in *our* flesh and spirits too: by our obeying it!

But the word used in verse 74 for "to serve" implies something more than menial obedience. It is a religious service, a particular devotion. It turns all our common life into a worship.

Without fear: serving this particular Lord grants us such protection that no enemy shall ever break through to destroy us. We need not fear the world. Moreover, *this* particular Lord does not oppress us into his service. We choose ("Let it be to me according to your word"). Neither, then, do we cringe and grin, serving because we fear *him*.

In holiness and righteousness: these are characteristics of a covenant people. The righteous are those who stand in a right relationship with God, trusting him above every created thing (above parents, spouses, one's own abilities, money) and performing with joy the requirements that come with this particular covenant (loving one another as Jesus has loved us). The holy, likewise, are those whose relationship with God separates them (even as God is separate) from the godless world. They neither serve the world nor take their identity from the world's standards, judgments, opinions, delights, behaviors. They are strangers here. But they are also, therefore, free and fearless!

Even so ought we to be when our Lord returns: a royal priesthood, a holy nation, God's own people.

∞

But how might we become that?

Why, turn to the Lord whom the Baptist proclaimed—and discover what God in him has already accomplished.

He has raised up for us a horn of salvation (v. 69). This "horn" is an image remembered from the Old Testament. A powerful ox establishes its four hoofs on the ground and raises its head, alert to danger, confident in its strength. With its head is raised the horn, which signifies, then, the might of the entire beast. That same horn, signifying victory, appeared on the helmets of warriors—and soon stood for the triumph of the Messianic king from the House of David. It also appeared on the corners of Israel's sacred altars, signs of the omnipotence of the Most High.

But the verb which Luke uses here for "raised up" is unusual. In the Old Testament it's commonly used as an act of God who "raises up" his people. In Luke's language it is used regarding Jesus, whom God has "raised up" from the dead (Acts 4:10–12)! So the early Christian church recognized that Jesus was himself the "horn of salvation." It is Jesus who makes the strength of God and the victory of his people real after all!

Turn unto him in order to turn into servants of the Lord, for in him is "the forgiveness of our sins" (v. 77). An Advent "turning to Jesus" requires three actions.

Let us seriously examine ourselves.

Let us genuinely confess the sins discovered within us, naming them before the altar and the horn of our salvation, Jesus.

Let us then fall completely upon "the tender mercy of our God" (v. 78). *Tender* means literally "the innermost parts of mercy," which *parts* are the heart, the lungs and the liver of a living body, the chambers of deepest emotion.

But these are God's innermost parts. Fall, then, upon the bosom of the Lord, whose mercy is as deep and as certain as his holy heart!

His forgiveness is likewise certain. It is his act, then, that shall raise you up again, his servant "all the days of your life."

Just as I am, thou wilt receive,
Wilt welcome, pardon, cleanse, relieve;
Because thy promise I believe,
   O Lamb of God, I come.

                              I come.

PART SIX

Joseph

Learn of Joseph:
The Character of Righteousness

LUKE 1:56

> *Mary stayed with Elizabeth about three months, and then returned to her home.*

MATTHEW 1:18–19

> *Now, the birth of Jesus Christ took place in this way:*
>
> *His mother Mary had been betrothed to Joseph; but before they came together, she was found to be with child—by the Holy Spirit.*
>
> *Joseph her husband was a just man, but was unwilling to put her to shame; so he resolved to divorce her quietly.*

JOSEPH, THE CARPENTER;

Joseph, a common man caught up in cosmic affairs;

Joseph, known to his neighbors, yet so unassuming that he sinks swiftly from biblical sight (indeed, this episode in Matthew is the single personal story by which we might really meet the man);

Joseph, more mute in the Gospels than Zechariah since the words of the latter are recorded in talk and in song, but of the former there are no words remembered, none;

Joseph, husband of Mary, adoptive father of Jesus—
Joseph is a just man.

Because the Evangelists say so little about him, each
word must bear enormous importance: Joseph is an
"upright" man. For raising his child, papa Joseph shall be
the very model of a righteous man—not so much in what
he says as in what he does.

So, let's examine it: what *does* he do? What is righteousness, as revealed in this brief episode of rights and
choices regarding the life of another?

Mary was found to be with child. . . .

Until the angel enlightens him with a holier explanation,
the evidence speaks for itself. Mary has committed adultery.
Betrothal binds two people as completely as marriage itself,
even though they don't yet live together or engage in sexual activity. So Mary has broken the Law, and the Law
defines the consequence.

The woman charged with so serious a crime as adultery
shall be stoned (Deut. 22:20–21).

But Joseph?

He resolved to divorce her quietly. He has some legal dis-
cretion here, and he chooses, Joseph *chooses*, not to accuse
her of the crime, neither publicly nor privately. He will make
no accusation at all, though he has every *right* to do so.

Evidently, one's rights do not define one's righteousness!

So this is what that righteous man is not: he is not self-
centered! If Joseph suffers a blow to his ego, his masculin-
ity, his stallion pride, we don't see it. He shows no anger, no
public outrage, no withering scorn. He doesn't pull a gun
on her. He doesn't beat her. He doesn't launch a campaign
to smear her. He never says, "She owes me" or "She'll pay
for this," as if her sin owes something to *him*. Mary's adul-

tery seems to have absolutely nothing to do with his reputation! And the righteous man does not view justice as something *he* receives for damages.

But today, in systems of law that ignore God altogether, and in hearts too filled with selves, folks demand justice as their own due! "She'll pay for this" means "*I'll* get that pay!" And we seek punishment to satisfy nothing but ourselves.

And Joseph?

He resolved to divorce her.... Though he chooses to do it quietly, he nevertheless chooses to divorce her.

Neither, then, is the righteous man the romantic hero who flouts laws and traditions for the sake of some higher individuality. Just as Joseph's decision doesn't center on himself, so it does not center on Mary or on their relationship as if that were the true nobility of humanity.

Joseph does not cry "Love conquers all!" He cannot make a small world of himself and his true love alone. He won't (as do so many today) exchange the restraints of God and one's culture for sweet, explosive emotions or for some fierce individuality that knows better than all the ancestors and all the parents combined.

No, Joseph's righteousness (1) honors God and God's will above the will of the self and even above the love of another. But it (2) is tempered by mercy.

Joseph resolves to keep the law, yes, but with such lenience that Mary's life will not be destroyed in the process. There will be no accusation, no trial at all (though a trial by ordeal is indicated where no witnesses can be found, cf. Num. 5:11–31), no public shame, nothing save the writ of divorce and two witnesses.

What, then, is righteousness? These two things: the obedience we owe to God and the mercy God grants us to grant others. It looks first to God, second to the other, never to the self—yet the self experiences a most holy peace in these relationships.

Come Lord Jesus:

Come, live in my heart as you lived in the house of Joseph. I yearn to be as righteous as he. O Lord, become the source of righteousness in me.

Amen

Learn of God:
Four Gifts of Christmas

MATTHEW 1:20–23

> *Now, as he was considering this, behold, an angel of the Lord appeared to Joseph in a dream, saying, "Joseph, son of David, do not be afraid to take Mary as your wife into your home, for the child conceived in her is of the Holy Spirit. She will give birth to a son, and you will call his name Jesus, for he will save his people from their sins."*
>
> *All this took place to fulfill what the Lord had spoken by the prophet who said,*
> *"Behold, a virgin shall conceive and bear a son;*
> *They'll call his name Immanuel, (meaning God with us)."*

BUT RIGHTEOUSNESS is never enough!

Yes, Joseph is a just man. And yes, his justice is tempered by mercy, so that Mary's good name need not be ruined. But justice alone would lead to separation. One man right, one woman wrong, and nothing left between them, neither life nor love nor family—and no child!

Truly, righteousness can create and maintain good order among us. Righteousness will protect the rights and the lives and the properties of individuals. Righteousness defines duties and obligations and privileges. It punishes deviance, purges crime, keeps the social body in health. All this is good and very good. But it is not good enough!

Righteousness may create good order—but it cannot *re*-create the people so that goodness and order arise from them.

It maintains society by restraining individual sin—but cannot *change* the individual from sinner to saint!

Something else is required. Something greater than humanity even at its best. Some act so completely divine that no human can ever take the credit: humanity can only take the benefit, for this act must be a gift, pure gift of God.

This act?—this something else? Why, it's Christmas!

Look how an angel astonishes the man in his sleep. (Sleep always signifies how perfectly passive is the receiver: God is the only one active now.) The angel reinterprets the woman's condition not as her sin but as God's grace: for as this sleeping man has had nothing to do with the pregnancy, so *no* man anywhere nor any human activity at all could have caused it. The woman is a virgin. God is the only actor now.

The angels says: *The child conceived in her is of the Holy Spirit*. The Spirit of God that brooded over the first creation is again at work, causing something as original as that, introducing into the world the Word by which the world was first created! This is grace beyond all righteousness, the gift of Christmas.

And this "child," says the angel, this "son" shall *be* a thing, and this "son" shall *do* a thing.

What shall he be? *Immanuel*: the presence of holy God among us, in space and time and human community. Our righteousness has not earned this. We have not enticed God here by sweetness, lovableness, goodness, faithfulness, prayers, kneelings, pieties, manifest obediences. *Immanuel* is here on his own recognizance, according to his own lights and his love.

And what shall he do? *Jesus*: he shall save his people from their sins. Our natural sinfulness and all our actual sins are the reasons we could never earn the presence of God among us. In fact, we should be as terrified of *Immanuel* as any fraud is of the truth. But this is the gift that righteousness could never accomplish, that Jesus himself, in coming among us, changes us, making us worthy of his presence, sisters and brothers of the Firstborn of God.

Even a man as just as Joseph should be terrified to be caught up by the cosmic forces that have already snatched his betrothed. But the angel says, *Do not be afraid to take Mary as your wife into your home.* And by grace he is not afraid.

And that is the third part of this Christmas gift which is beyond all righteousness: (1) In Jesus God is made present to humanity. (2) Jesus changes us, removing anything that would sever us from God, making us children of his Father. (3) And no fear shall overcome us as nearer and nearer God comes to us. We shall desire the intimacy and delight in it.

No, we shall not fear. Rather, we shall discover within us—as did Joseph when he awoke—the miraculous ability to obey the voice of God.

And that is the fourth gift of Christmas, the consequence of the first three, surprising enough to deserve its own meditation:

Righteousness renewed in us after all!

Come, Lord Jesus:

Come near me. Come, change my sinful nature. Come to me, then, as my brother. Remove all fear from my trembling heart, and make your baby bed within me, where you become all my righteousness and all I need to recommend me to the Father, now and forevermore.

Amen

DECEMBER TWENTY-ONE

An Exaltation:
The Fourth Gift, Goodness!

MATTHEW 1:24–25

> *When Joseph awoke from his sleep, he did as the*
> *angel of the Lord commanded him. He took his wife*
> *home, but he had no sexual relations with her until she*
> *had borne a son, and he called his name Jesus.*

T HE DAY BEFORE YESTERDAY we begged for a righteousness like Joseph's, that selfless obedience to God which is tempered with mercy toward humanity.

Yesterday we realized that our righteousness alone could never repair the covenant between ourselves and the Lord. Mercifully, God himself initiated that repair with the gift of Jesus, who "finished" it on the cross.

Today our Christmas grows merry, almost giddy, in the discovery of an irony: that the righteousness for which we strove so hard and so failingly suddenly appears within us after all, but as a gift!

O my love, we *can* be good! Good without some sneaking guilt that we're deceiving ourselves. Good without a grinning, offensive arrogance. Good and humble and grateful at once. Good and knowing the goodness. Good, good, and glad in it!

For this is not *self*-righteousness. It is the righteousness of God. Its source is God and not ourselves. It comes near us in Immanuel. And it flows into us through Jesus who "will save his people from their sins," Jesus whom God made to be sin "so that in him we might become the righteousness of God" (2 Cor. 5:21). It's a gift, the consequence of our salvation.

It is like laughter, the hilarity of God—a grand, celestial irony. For in the moment of our salvation, in precisely that moment when we are no longer required to keep the laws of God, lo: we *can!* Nope, don't need to. But yep, we're able!

Now, therefore, we turn to the Ten Commandments without fear of failure. Nor do we feel oppressed by the law. Nor does the law cause a loss of personal liberty. No, we *want* to keep it. It is our will, in harmony with God's will.

O my dear, obedience unto God is now our glad thanksgiving for the gifts of Christmas. Obedience is that highest, most noble human accomplishment: honor for God, the creature's cry of love for its Creator. We, the obedient—we are artists of the divine. We, the righteous—divinity dwells in us and in the sight of all creation.

So we are like Joseph after all.

At the advent of the Lord within our lives, we waken from our long sleep of sin's separations.

The invitation is ringing still in our ears: *Don't be afraid. Come, join the cosmic drama wherein heaven and humanity meet in the tiny person of a baby.*

Take Mary home. Honor the one who bears your Lord to you. Commit your life and all your ways to them—yea, even as if you had married them.

And name him Jesus. Recognize in him the salvation for humankind, then announce it abroad by naming the name.

Arise and obey me.

And this, Christian, becomes the fourth gift of our Christmas, that we *do*. We can. Joseph "did as the angel of the Lord commanded him; he took his wife home."

Come, Lord Jesus!

You are my righteousness. You are my goodness, the cause and the reason for goodness. You are my life and the light of life. You are my love and all my loving. You are the most noble language I ever can utter, my words and all their meaning, my wisdom, my truth, and the better part of my self.

Come, and I shall be whole.

Amen

PART SEVEN

Jesus

The Story:
Going Up to Bethlehem

LUKE 2:1–4

> *In those days a decree went out from Caesar Augustus that all the world should be enrolled. This was the first enrollment, when Quirinius was governor of Syria.*
>
> *And all went to be enrolled, each to his own city.*
>
> *And Joseph also went up from Galilee, from the city of Nazareth, to Judea, to the city of David, which is called Bethlehem, because he was of the house and lineage of David.*

HUSH, NOW. Here is the core of the story. It begins in earnest. The earth is turning toward the birthing of its king. The heavens have started their slow spiral down, down to a Judean town. In an instant in eternity, in the space inside a manger both shall meet like fingers touching.

Governments and peoples, too, are entoiled in the measureless event—though ignorantly, since the company of those who know what God is doing is humble still, and very small.

Governments and peoples, yes, and *all the world*.

All the world.

The emperor Octavian, whom the people call "Augustus" (the sublime one, consecrated and divine); the emperor

Octavian, whose other name, Caesar, will grow so grand as to embrace world rulers for millennia hence, Czars and Kaisers—the emperor is unwittingly involved. He decrees a worldly thing, and heaven smiles.

All went to be enrolled. . . .

Then, vastly, humanity itself begins to move, wheels in wheels turning, tribes and tongues and peoples and nations—all caught in the momentum of heavenly revolutions, but unaware. They are moving absently, their heads bent down like oxen at the mill wheel.

Oh, what a puzzlement are the populations of this dark earth! They know not the nearness of God. They elevate their emperors to the status of the divine; but at the descent of true Divinity they go about their business unaware.

Nevertheless, they go, and their business is heaven's business in spite of all, because God loves them! God loves them, and *that's* the reason for the grand migrations of heaven and earth toward one another in order to meet and marry in the birth of a baby.

Vastly, humanity is moving, while angels as silent as snow fall down from heaven. The peoples are rivers flowing uphill, *up from Galilee to Judea*.

And here is the precious center of all these universal turnings: a man and a woman are climbing a winding path to Bethlehem. No one notices. They are lowly and all too common. It is evening. They make a small silhouette against the fiery sky.

Long, long have they been traveling. The journey began two thousand years ago when the Lord said to Abraham, *In you all the families of the earth shall be blessed*.

The woman knows when the journey began. Even now as she labors uphill she sings the soft song in her heart,

He is helping his servant Israel
  Remembering the mercy
  He uttered to our fathers,
Abraham and his posterity, forever.

The woman knows. Though no one else in all the world may know, yet she knows:

The life inside her is about to become the life of the world.

Ah, but hush. Hush now, my best beloved. For that ancient journey, and the turnings together of heaven and earth, and the imminent collisions of angels and peoples— why, it all began the day before yesterday, when governments decreed enrollments and Joseph and Mary packed a bag in Nazareth and started walking south, to Bethlehem, to the dawning.

O Lord!

  And I know it, too! Mary may go calmly toward her Christmas, but I am filled with excitement for mine. O my Lord, God of the little and of the large, your love is as universal as all creation, and yet as particular as my small heart! Here at Christmas, you embrace the nations. Whether they know it, whether they confess it or not, you, Jesus, have saved all people from their sins!

  But you are the baby in my cradle, here in my house and under my tree. How can such impossibilities be?

  But with God nothing (I know, I know) shall be impossible.

                                        Hallelujah!

O Mary, Virgin Mother:
May I Walk with You a While?

LUKE 2:5

> *Joseph went up from Galilee to Bethlehem to be enrolled with Mary, his betrothed, who was great with child.*

SOON, SOON. The exertion of the journey has already triggered some irregular contractions. The baby dropped several days ago and lies low on the floor of Mary's pelvis. Last week she could scarcely breathe. Today she can't hold her water. When the donkey steps roughly, she giggles and shakes her head.

Soon.

Tomorrow?

Mary has felt it even from its fluttering beginnings. Joseph has seen and touched it. For months, the parents with shining eyes have experienced the life inside of her, and sometimes they've wept, and sometimes they've burst out laughing, and sometimes she simply closes her eyes and giggles.

But that life is so big now. Huge and slung so low.

Once while Mary was bathing, Joseph noticed some bone jut from the side of her abdomen. He shouted astonishment: a heel, perhaps. An elbow. It seemed the baby wanted to punch his way out. Joseph began to laugh. Whatever bone it was, it didn't withdraw again, but moved along the equator of the mother's belly, driving her eyebrows up. She gasped, then joined the laughter of her husband. Shining eyelashes, wet with tears.

But the baby has filled all the womb-space, now. He's big. His head's at the door. He wants to come! He wants to be born.

Tomorrow? Will tomorrow bring the dayspring from on high?

Mary's belly is a globe as round as the great earth, and very full. Full of the gathering of God. God's presence, God's populations.

Well, consider: her fullness is that "fullness of time . . . when God sends forth his son, born of a woman, born under the law to redeem those who were born under the law, so that we might receive adoption as children of God." Therefore, "God has sent the Spirit of his son into our hearts, crying *Abba! Father!*" (Gal. 4:4–7).

O Mary, virgin Mother, that's the Son of God inside of you, straining soon, soon to be born.

O Mary, in a sacred way a nation, too, now fills your womb; for in the conception of your Son is the conceiving of the whole Church that is to be, all its members, every baby voice that will learn with Jesus to call God *Abba*, "Papa! Papa!"

O Mary, great with child, you are great with myriads of myriads. They shall come forth as black as a midnight Africa, blue-white as the ice of Sweden, noble and troubled and humble and crooked, mute and versed in ten thousand tongues, poets and fishers, the fat, the fast, the fool, the funny. They shall defy all categories except this one, that they will be sisters and brothers of the Son inside you now, all of them "born not of blood nor of the will of the flesh nor of the will of a man, but of God" (John 1:13).

O Mary, virgin Mother, groaning toward Bethlehem, thinking of nothing but birth and obedience, may I walk with you a while before the borning? May I, my meditations, bear something of the burden? May I labor with you today and tomorrow toward Bethlehem?

For in a sacred manner, you are my mother—and very soon, at the delivery of your Holy Son, I shall be delivered too.

O love of God that fell on a Maiden
  Soft as dew on the flower,
Pour on me your storming power;
Rain on me to change my pagan
  Heart into your bower.

O Son of God who filled the Maiden
  With your holy seed,
Plant your presence here in me:
I, whose life is almost faded,
  Seek a new nativity:

As you were born on Christmas Eve
  All sinners to receive,
So let me, Lord, be born again
And I will cry, Amen! Amen!
  Unto the end.

The Story:
The Holy, Human Birth

LUKE 2:6–7

> *And so it was that while they were there, the days were accomplished that she should be delivered. And she brought forth her first-born son and wrapped him in swaddling clothes and laid him in a manger, because there was no room for them in the inn.*
>
> *On this night it all comes true.*
> *Every song receives its meaning.*
> *All the promises are kept.*
> *The Lord of glory makes a doorway*
> *Of the Virgin's tender flesh,*
> *And comes, and slumbers in a crèche.*

TONIGHT OUR ADVENT anticipations are over. Christ arrives. God enters creation as every human ever has—but though the way is common, it is God who takes that way tonight, so the birth is uncommon indeed, a crack in the universe, and the baby blazes with divinity.

Ah, but the baby's a baby, after all. And he's born in a stall, the tethering of animals—so who's to know the difference? Mary. Joseph. Those who heard and believed the promises. Those who sang the songs of Advent. Me. You.

It's Christmas Eve. By faith we, too, are present, watching.

Mary is a teenager, younger than my daughter. But the task at hand makes a woman of her. Watch:

She whispers, and Joseph makes sheaves of clean straw. Some he piles in a steep backrest; with some he surrounds a deeper scoop of looser straw; over all he drapes a woolen blanket, and Mary lowers herself onto the place prepared for her. Listen:

Her groanings never surrender to pain. Nor does her posture crumple beneath it. Rather, pain swells below her like an ocean, and whenever a great wave heaves upward, threatening to swamp her, Mary concentrates and rides the pain; rides high the swell as if in a boat of her own strong will; feels it, certainly; suffers the iron contractions; but never loses control; and down the other side she rows, to breathe a while before the next wave rises and rolls. Watch:

Suddenly Mary's whole torso snaps forward, catching her eyes by surprise. No utterance now. No breathing at all. She stares as if the earth has opened at her toes. Her teeth gleam in the darkness, shaping a silent, grinning scream. Her forehead flashes sweat. Suddenly there are several sounds in quick succession. Listen!

A slurping—a moist release—and the soft crushings of dry straw.

A deep-throated sigh, a nearly animal grunt, and puffing.

A man's voice, drawing breath and sobbing.

For in the scoop of the woolen blanket lies a trembling infant, a little corpus streaked with the fluids of his mother's womb.

Jesus.

Joseph picks up the tiny baby so that his mother can see him. She smiles a radiant smile. Her face becomes bright corona. The father is thick-fingered. The baby's head lolls left and right. The mother reaches as if to catch the babe. She gathers the tiny life into her bosom and kisses and kisses and kisses the blue flesh, until Jesus wails in a cricket voice and the blood enriches his face. But watch:

Suddenly Mary thrusts the baby back to Joseph and bends to push a second thing out of her body, the afterbirth still trailing the baby's umbilical. And compulsively Joseph is wiping Jesus clean. Then, together, they cut the cord. And soon on this holy night, mother Mary is wrapping her baby tightly in the swaddling cloths, kissing, kissing him.

She is tired, now. The baby too is tired. It has been hard work, this quiet arrival of salvation.

Mary lays Jesus on clean straw in a wooden trough. For just a moment she places the knuckles of three fingers against the baby's cheek. Then she closes her eyes and sighs and becomes a teenager again. And sleeps.

Joseph sits watch. As do we.

It is Christmas Eve. Jesus is among us now. Oh, how right and quiet is everything in all the world, for the gift has been given. Oh, how peaceful are we.

> *Silent night. Holy night.*
> *All is calm, all is bright,*
> *Round yon Virgin Mother and child.*
> *Holy infant so tender and mild,*
> *Sleep in heavenly peace.*
> *Sleep in heavenly peace.*

Christmas Day:
Our Door to the Nativity

LUKE 2:8–14

> *And there were in the same country shepherds abiding in the field, keeping watch over their flock by night.*
>
> *And, lo, the angel of the Lord came upon them, and the glory of the Lord shone round about them, and they were sore afraid.*
>
> *But the angel said unto them, "Fear not, for, behold, I bring you good tidings of great joy, which shall be to all people. For unto you is born this day in the city of David a Savior, which is Christ the Lord. And this shall be a sign unto you: Ye shall find the babe wrapped in swaddling clothes and lying in a manger."*
>
> *And suddenly there was with the angel a multitude of the heavenly host praising God and saying:*
>
> *"Glory to God in the highest,*
> *And peace to his people on earth!"*

IT'S CHRISTMAS DAY. The quietness is shattered. God will never, never be silent again! And now the world must know the news.

So here comes Gabriel again. Get ready for more singing.

But this time the angel grows bright before a bunch of nameless folk. First it was Zechariah, next Mary, next Joseph, all of whom had roles to play in the coming of the Christ—but now . . . shepherds! How many? Don't know. And these aren't even the owners of the sheep; they're the working stiffs who pulled a night watch. So what are these people in the order of things? How do they rate such invitations to the great banquet of the King?

Well, they rate because they rate! They are chosen because God chooses them. It has nothing to do with what they have done. And it clearly can't be who they are—unless "who they are" is nothing at all, for this same Jesus whom they will rush to worship shall fill his own feast hall with the poor and maimed and lame and blind, with those who travel the highways and lurk in hedges (Luke 14). The Lord God and the Lord in human flesh—they have the same notions, you see.

So here comes Gabriel again, and what he says is, "Good tidings of great joy . . . for all people!"

Well, of course. That's why the shepherds are first: they represent *all* the nameless, *all* the working stiffs, the great wheeling population of the whole world.

That's how we got to the birthing last night, you and I. Zechariah and Mary and Elizabeth and Joseph and John: each is a particular person with a very particular relationship to Jesus. They may act as models for us. We can try to imitate them. But we cannot *be* them. They occupy places of distinct privilege, and there simply is not room in their skins for any besides themselves.

But the shepherds, now—these people without names or position or repute or privilege—we need not merely be *like* them. We can *be* them. They *are* us in the story. Name one with your own name. Give her your history and your face. Enter his place in midnight on the chilly fields near Bethlehem.

So here comes Gabriel to us, interrupting our common labors.

So we are the ones frightened by this sudden burst of immediate divinity. Our stomachs contract. Our hands fly up in front of our faces. We had expected holiness to appear in Church, perhaps—but not at work.

To us, then, in our own ears the angel says, "Don't be afraid." The angel proves the miracle of his presence by removing fear and uncertainty and by giving us the ability truly to listen to him. And this to our hearing hearts is what he says:

"Your Savior is born. Your Savior is here and very near. Nevermore shall you be ignorant of God and God's deep love for you, because I will give you signs for finding that love. Look, he is a baby, wrapped in plain baby clothing, lying in the humblest of homes, a manger.

"Look: the beams of his stable will become the beams of a cross, and as he is born human, so shall he a human die. True death: a death like yours.

"But as he is also born the Son of God, so shall his death also kill the sin and everything that separates you from the throne of God. True death, the truest death: the death of death itself."

Above us, then, the stars of the night sky whirl and whirl and come spiraling down. And the closer they come and the brighter they grow, the more we see that every star is a choral member of the hosts of God, and all the stars together are singing, *Glory, gloria!* and we are not afraid. Tremendous are their voices, wild the light erupting around us. The earth trembles like the skin of a drum. *Glory, gloria!*

they cry, for their song embraces all that the Lord has begun this day: *Glory to God in the highest of heavens! And peace to the people with whom he is pleased!*

And who are these people? With whom does the good Lord choose to take his pleasure?

The shepherds.

The plain and nameless—

—whose every name the Lord knows very well.

You.

And me.

Merry Christmas, my best beloved. Merry Christmas, child.

Now sing we, now rejoice; now raise to heaven
  our voice;
He from whom joy streameth poor in a manger lies;
Not so brightly beameth the sun in yonder skies.
Thou my Savior art! Thou my Savior art.

Come from on high to me; I cannot rise to thee.
Cheer my wearied spirit, O pure and holy child;
Through thy grace and merit, blest Jesus, Lord
  most mild,
Draw me unto thee! Draw me unto thee.

Now through his Son doth shine the Father's
  grace divine.
Death o'er us had reigned through sin and vanity;
He for us obtained eternal joy on high.
May we praise him there! May we praise him there.

(*In dulci iubilo*, c. 1300, anonymous;
tr. Arthur T. Russell, 1851)

An Exaltation:
Jesus, Here We Come!

LUKE 2:16

> *And they came with haste and found Mary and Joseph and the babe lying in a manger.*

WE ARE THE SHEPHERDS who run: from the fields to the stable, from the night to the morning, from our labors to the Lord.

We are the ones who run this year, too, as in every year past:

From toil and our daily chores, we run to the comfort in Bethlehem.

From our obligations and responsibilities, we run to the strength of Immanuel: God's strong arm among us.

From our fears of loss and instability, from the anguish of troubled finances, from poverty we run to the treasure that will not tarnish nor ever diminish, the baby's eyes like coins in our purse, the baby's eyes eternal.

From our obscurity; from the darkness in which we live our lives, unacknowledged, inglorious; from our truer condition as "no one, people that are not" we run to the Son of God, who knows each of our names, and who will call us by our names, and whose very call will empower us to follow.

From sorrow we run to joy.

From hatreds we run to love.

From antagonisms we run to peace.

From sickness we run to the healer.

From sin we run to the Savior.

From death we run to life.

O child, we kneel before you. We have no gifts, neither the gold of riches nor the frankincense of holy aroma, nor the myrrh of salve and embalmment. We must ourselves *be* the gifts we bring to you. Jesus, we offer our bodies as living sacrifices; let them be holy and acceptable to you.

Son of Mary and Son of God, we worship you. There is no one more worthy than you. In you we see the mercies of God.

O Word by which the whole Creation came to be, we come to you in rags and tags and unembarrassed, because you, too, have chosen not royalty nor wealth nor power but the lowly existence of shepherds. Swaddled and laid in a manger, you are like us. We yearn to be like you.

O little Jesus, sleep. Sleep while we kneel and watch over you in a dim light this Christmas too. We honor the woman that bore you. We admire the man that adopted you. We maintain sweet memories of those who brought us, like Mary and Joseph, into the stable to worship you during our own Christmases past. But you are the one we praise. You are the one whom we trust. In you we rest. In you we place our faith. Forever and forever, you are the Christ—and you are our Lord forever.

Hush, mother Mary; we'll watch for you.
Sleep while your baby is sleeping too.

He is a lamb both tender and young,
We will be shepherds to shepherd your son.

After his infancy, after his sleep,
He'll be the shepherd and we'll be the sheep.

O Mary, we'll see to his happiness
Before his Father requires a death.

Then he will call us by our names
And lead us all like little lambs
  Home.

Learn of the Shepherds:
Five Stages of Faith

LUKE 2:15–20

> *And it came to pass, as the angels were gone away from them into heaven, the shepherds said one to another, "Let us now go even unto Bethlehem, and see this thing which is come to pass, which the Lord hath made known unto us."*
>
> *And they came with haste, and found Mary and Joseph and the babe lying in a manger.*
>
> *And when they had seen it, they made known abroad the saying which was told them concerning this child. And all they that heard it wondered at those things which were told them by the shepherds.*
>
> *But Mary kept all these things and pondered them in her heart.*
>
> *And the shepherds returned, glorifying and praising God for all the things that they had heard and seen, as it was told unto them.*

DIVIDE ME INTO five parts, then put me back together again. Five parts: the ears, the feet, the eyes. The tongue as a teller of truth—and finally, for the music of my heart, my singing voice.

O Jesus, this night I have given you the whole of me. Tiny baby, you have purchased me. I am yours.

I am the shepherd who came to see you in your manger, and I am the one who left with you in my heart.

I am the nameless, the universal example of all who encounter you and leave believing. In me might anyone see the stages by which faith begins.

My ears first heard the news of you, who you are and what you'll do. It was an angel told me. Whenever this message comes down from heaven, whoever the messenger, he becomes an angel, for the message makes him so. Hearing the good news, I went from fear to fascination.

And hearing it, I had to emerge from my familiar, habitual ways and move to the place where you are. I rose on my own *two feet* and, by search and by desiring, I sought the signs of your presence: the swaddling cloths of the rebirth of those who love you; the genuine meekness of a manger-existence—for in such lives do you still lie. I sought the Mary-face of those who serve you with willingness and joy, and the Joseph-hand of the just.

I ran in darkness and in the night.

But I found you.

My eyes, my own eyes, have seen you.

> *I had heard of thee by the hearing of the ear,*
> *but now my eye see thee;*
> *Therefore I despise myself,*
> *and repent in dust and ashes.*

So spoke Job (42:5–6) when he was confronted by the prodigious power and the terrible righteousness of the Creating Deity. Job's created self was burned to ash. Likewise

Isaiah, in the presence of the glory of the Lord, cried, "Woe is me! I am lost!"

But unto me, dear Jesus, you appear in a flesh like mine—and that is the measure of your love *for* me: how low you come is how high you love! Both are infinite.

I come to you and I see a baby: righteous, yes; glorious, yes; but a form that does not separate us on account of my scoundrel nature—a form, rather, that draws us together in spite of it.

I see you and though the sight should make me ashes, I do not die! That makes this life new and gracious altogether. I see you, I see light, I see heavenly love. Such seeing, so intimate, is relationship immediately. Such seeing *is* believing.

Oh, how could I ever keep silent about this wonderful deed? You have called me out of darkness into your marvelous light!

My tongue must tell what my mind knows well. I must make known what the angels told me, because I've seen their saying! I must myself become the angel of this message, until all wonder at what I tell them, until Mary your mother grows quiet in contemplations of your person, Jesus.

And even now my heart is in my throat—and that is my fifth part, wholly given unto you, O Lord: my singing *voice*. For as I return to the regions of my past life (which will change for the change in me) I am glorifying and praising God for all I've heard and seen, as it was told to me.

This is Christmas: that I saw in flesh the Word through whom the world was made, but I did not die. I saw the very source of life, the light that bedazzles the darkness, and I was not blinded. Rather, I who in darkness could not see have now received my sight. I see! I see—and that is the gift of my Christmas.

O Jesus Christ,
Thy manger is
My paradise at which my soul reclineth.
For there, O Lord,
Doth lie the Word
Made flesh for us; herein thy grace forth shineth.

He whom the sea
And wind obey
Doth come to serve the sinner in great meekness.
Thou, God's own Son,
With us art one,
Dost join us and our children in our weakness.

Thou Christian heart,
Who-e'er thou art,
Be of good cheer and let no sorrow move thee!
For God's own Child,
In mercy mild,
Joins thee to Him; how greatly God must love thee!

(Paul Gerhardt, 1653)

O My Lord,
I Love the Names by Which
We Know You

LUKE 2:21

Eight days later, when the time came to circumcise the child, he was called Jesus, the name given by the angel before he was conceived in the womb.

CHILD, ON THE EIGHTH day of your life they name you; heaven and earth together name you, angels of fire, parents of dust—and pilgrims like me are granted to use the name as well: past and present and forever, you come to the call of your name.*

It is a name almighty and completely unique, since there is no other name under heaven by which we may be saved. Yes, and it's the common name by which your family will call you to supper. Earthly entities, too, will use it to record you, to address you, to condemn you:

Jesus.

Child, your name is Jesus.

Joshua. *Yehoshuah.* "Yahweh Will Save."

---

*The Christian Church celebrates the naming of Jesus always on the eighth day of his life: January 1.

And so shall I call you with humble gratitude. It is a sign of the joining of heaven and earth in your sole self. It signifies the perfect association of ordinary and extraordinary, your human and your heavenly origins. In you the antipodes become one. Little children will lisp, "Jesus loves me, this I know . . . ," while others facing death will be emboldened by that name.

But *Jesus* is not the only name by which the world will know you. In fact, the Christmas story grants us at least six others, each one touching some other aspect of your person—and each a gift. For when in prayer I use your other names, by them is our relationship enriched.

And here are those the angel uttered:

(1) *Savior* is how the pagans entitled their emperors, those whom they begged to protect them from enemies and famine and thieves and early perishings. But you do what the rulers of clay could not. You save us truly from Satan and Sickness and Sin and Death.

(2) *Son of God* referred to the heroes of Greek and Roman antiquity, people like Heracles so good and moral that the gods received them into heaven at their deaths. Likewise, Julius Caesar was declared "God Manifest," the "Savior" of humankind. Two years after he died, they named him *divis Julius*, "divine Julius." What could his adopted son, Caesar Augustus, be called, then, but *divi filius*, "Son of the Divine" and "Son of God"?

All this expresses the deepest yearning of humanity— true insofar as all people everywhere desire some divine contact. People yearn for a goodness that *can* receive a heavenly reward, a goodness which is in the end immortal. Thus, apart from you "Son of God" is true in the universality of human imaginings—

—but it is truly true, historically true, effectively and pragmatically true only in you, sweet Jesus. You are our divine contact, and your goodness alone is immortal—but it becomes my goodness too when I call upon your name!

There is no other God but God, and no Son of God but you.

Therefore we call you (3) *Immanuel* and (4) *Christ*, the "anointed one" of God, the *Messiah* finally arriving among us. You are the fulfillment of human hope for holy leadership! You are the (5) *King* of the kingdom coming, more glorious than David of the kingdom gone: eternal, where David died; and where David shed the blood of others to obtain a national peace, you yourself will bleed for the peace of our souls.

And (6) *Lord*. We call you Lord. It is, in fact, the very first creed of the Christian Church: "Jesus is my Lord" (Phil. 2:11). But it bears a tender, relational meaning too. For in Old English the leader of a tribe was called the *Hlaf-Weard*, two words stuck together: *Hlaf* is our word "loaf." It means bread. *Weard* is our word "Ward." It means keeping. The leader was the "Keeper of the Bread," the one who doled food evenly and wisely that none should die even in tough times. Now, *Hlaf-weard* over the centuries became *Hlaford*, then, *Loverd*, and finally, *Lord*.

You are my bread-keeper, Jesus. You feed me all I need, body and soul. You are the food of my Holy Communion. The bread that you keep is yourself, for the life of all who believe in you.

⚜

The Many Names of the Blessed One

Ah, Master, I will use them.
Rabboni, I will pray.
Good Shepherd, I will not abuse them
However far I stray.

Redeemer, you have bought me
Back from slavery.
How could I scorn the Son that taught me
Light and how to see?

This day of circumcision,
This covenantal day,
Names you our future Resurrection
Life and Truth and Way.

Ah, baby, head so heavy,
Lay it down, I pray.
Soon you will raise it strong and steady
For the crown of Christ in Glory—
Perpetual Christmas Day!

PART EIGHT

Simeon and Anna

The Story:
Ascending to the Temple

LUKE 2:22–24

> *Now when the time came for their purification according to the Law of Moses, the parents brought Jesus up to Jerusalem to present him to the Lord (as it is written in the Law of the Lord: "Every male child who opens the womb will be called holy to the Lord")— and to offer a sacrifice according to what is dictated in the Law of the Lord: "A pair of turtledoves or two young pigeons."*

MARY'S BABY IS forty days old plus one. His eyes have grown bright. Even before his circumcision they had learned to focus; swiftly they found his parents' faces, causing smiles in both of them—smiles that triggered smiles in Jesus. Mary's baby smiles when he sees his mother. Such a good baby!

And Mary is rich with milk. The nursing infant tugs and swallows and breathes in the rhythms of a long-distance runner. She presses a finger against her breast-flesh beneath the baby's nose: a passageway for air. He gazes up into her eyes. There are moments when she cannot stand the pleasure and the mystery of this motherly exchange. It grips her womb. It fills her soul to bursting. She hurts with the goodness, and she weeps. The baby releases her nipple and produces an open-mouthed grin, milk-drool running round his gums.

It is his forty-first day of life.

It is also the first day since his birth that his mother is ritually clean and free to enter the courts of the Temple.

So when Jesus has drunk his fill, Mary washes him and wraps him for a morning's walk, and the small family sets out over the stony hills toward Jerusalem.

The baby nods in the sunlight and dozes.

The same bright sun reveals how young his mother is. Her face is roundish still from the pregnancy, her mouth silly with smiling. She is going up to the Temple to make an offering for her ritual purification. All is well.

There! Joseph touches his wife's elbow. She lifts her eyes and sees the walls of Jerusalem and the hills above them, Zion to the left, the Mount of Olives to the right, and the Temple between. Joseph has been here before. She hasn't. Her breathing quickens.

As they approach, the wall hides the holy places, but then they enter by a southeastern gate, and Mary looks up— up the steps before her, up the street that rises higher than the steps, up to the Royal Porches on the near side of the Temple Mount, up, up even to the Temple itself.

Jesus wakes and squawks. Poor baby! Mary, transported by the sight before her, has been squashing the infant.

Higher even than the Temple is the smoke of sacrifice, ascending to the nostrils of God. She cannot hear the hissing of the meat, but Mary can smell it. She grins her own drooling grin, dumbstruck with the wonder of the worship of God. All is well.

Joseph leads her up the stairs and up the street and through the Temple gates and among the columns of the

Royal Porches, where merchants are selling animals for offering.

If they had money, Mary would surely honor the law and buy a lamb and a pigeon. But the Laws of Moses make provision for those too poor to purchase a lamb.

How good of God!

Mary touches Joseph's elbow, now, and points at two rock pigeons in a basket cage, whispering, "He fills the hungry with good things."

Joseph buys the pigeons.

Together—mother and father and the little baby—they walk out into sunlight again, entering the Court of the Women. People, the people of God and Mary's own people, move about upon the pavement. She and Joseph are walking slowly toward the Nicanor Gate on the west side of this court. It gives way to the Court of Israel, where her husband may enter, though she may not; and he will bring a priest to her at the gate; and she will proffer her little sacrifice for purification. . . .

Suddenly Mary turns and presses her face into the robes of Joseph's chest. She cannot hug him. She's holding the baby. But she bursts into great, loud, heaving sobs, so he puts his arms around them both and pats her back. He keeps patting her back. He does not know what's wrong.

But nothing is wrong. Everything is right! Impossibly perfect, so treacherously *right* that Mary can't bear it.

All is well. All manner of thing is very well, and her tears are the gratitude of a soul now spilling over.

But there's the smallest tug of fear within her: however could such goodness last?

The baby grunts. His parents are pressing the breath right out of him.

And the old man approaching them from within the Court of Israel is not a priest.

O Christ:

In this world of time and mutability there come moments of perfect stillness, perfect peace—holy moments when everything is so absolutely right that time ceases and joy overcomes us. Then eternity breaks into time. Then we glimpse the truth of your love. We taste briefly the feast to come. And we are glad.

Keep us, O Lord, when these moments must pass, from forgetting them. Keep them, O Lord, within us as reminders already now to thank you for what shall surely be.

Amen

The Story:
The Prophets Prove Him the Messiah

LUKE 2:25–27, 36–38

> *Now there was in Jerusalem a man by the name of Simeon who was righteous and devout, looking for the consolation of Israel. The Holy Spirit was upon him; and it had been revealed to him by this Holy Spirit that he would not see death before he had seen the Lord's Messiah.*

> *Inspired by the Spirit, then, Simeon came into the Temple court. When the parents brought in Jesus to do for him what was customary according to the Law, Simeon embraced the child in his arms....*

> *And there was a prophetess, Anna daughter of Phanuel, of the tribe of Asher, who was of great age; for she had married as a young girl and lived with her husband seven years, and then by herself as a widow for eighty-four years. She never left the Temple courts. Day and night she worshiped God, fasting and praying.*

> *Now at this very moment she too came up and gave thanks to God, and she spoke about the child to all those waiting for the redemption of Jerusalem.*

So HERE COMES an old man through the Nicanor Gate. His fierce, moist eye is fixed on ... on Mary? No, but on the child in her arms. On Jesus—who now is wide awake, whose baby eyes catch hungrily at every Temple thing.

Old man, his head bound tight by a turban nearly as old as he: there is a glowing in him, like the dawning light. There is a pressure in him, like song about to burst.

The baby sees him, stares at him in return, and is not afraid.

But Mary's afraid. Joseph isn't acting like a shield now. And her ears are painfully alert.

Simeon, hiss several priests nearby. *Simeon, righteous and devout*, they whisper. To her it sounds like criticism: perhaps they hate the one who makes them feel inferior under the Law. But people said the same about her husband! What sort of soul is troubled by righteousness? Perhaps she shouldn't fear the old man's fierceness after all.

Ah, but he comes toward her like a storm wind sweeping the dry Esdraelon.

Simeon, the priests hiss. *Says he's won't die till he's seen the comfort of Israel. But "comfort, comfort" was promised long ago, and never yet has come. Let Messiah appear on a horse with a sword! Let him cut Rome at her throat and set us free. Then the old man can die, for then he will have seen the Lord's Anointed!*

Mary would close her ears if she could—but she's holding the baby, watching that old man bear down upon them. There's something invidious in this whispered language. Oh, shut my ears! What was so recently so right is suddenly twisted, distorted. Messiah on a horse? Messiah, an assassin?—the fist of a mighty force?

But the old man who's seeking the Christ—his rheumy eye is fixed on Jesus.

And Mary remembers the promise in Isaiah:

Comfort, comfort my people,
says your God.

Speak tenderly to Jerusalem,
   and cry to her
that her warfare is ended,
   that her iniquity is pardoned,
that she has received from the Lord's hand
   double for all her sins.
A voice cries in the wilderness:
   "Prepare the way of the Lord!"

"You! You," fierce Simeon cries as he arrives. "You are the one!"

He reaches for the child. In spite of her fears and confusion, his mother releases Jesus to Simeon.

The baby gazes into the red, watery eyes above him, unafraid.

"He'll never ride a war-horse," Mary announces spontaneously. "My child will never swing the death-sword!"

And the old man, his eyes trembling with a holy light, does not disagree. "Blessed be God," he cries, "for a Christ of the kinder consolations."

At that same moment Mary feels a hand on her shoulder. She turns and finds an ancient woman, short, more wrinkled than the hills of Judea.

"It's him," the woman says. "This child is the redemption of Jerusalem!"

Young Mary, crowded now by aging and age and the ages! She herself has fulfilled the Law, and here are two prophets proving that her baby truly is the Christ. (For in Luke it is always the Law and the Prophets who interpret Jesus [24:27], the Law and the Prophets whom Jesus fulfills [24:44].)

Simeon nods sharply at the ancient woman.

"Anna," he says.

"Simeon," says she.

Suddenly his old face splits in a grin. He elevates the infant between them and asks: "How many years?"

Jesus looks down on the ancient woman.

"As a widow, eighty-four years," says she. "I am one hundred and three—never not fasting, never not praying for this. Oh, thank the Lord," Anna whispers, reaching and brushing the face of the baby with one swollen knuckle. "Thank God for little Messiah here. No horse," she says in the ear of his mother. "No sword for his enemies, no. No warrior, this. No killer, he. Your baby is better than that."

It was then that the old man sang two songs in the courts of the Temple. One caused Mary unspeakable joy. The second one nearly killed her.

Jesus,

Whenever I wish your kingdom to progress by power, forgive me. Whenever I myself take up swords, political, commercial, physical—even and especially when I do so in your name—forgive me. Forgive my wish for a warrior Lord. Forgive my angers, my condemnations of others—of any others, whether I feel that I am the righteous one, or that they are too righteous for me.

Oh, Jesus, teach me what sort of Messiah you are. Save me from seeking a human heroism in you, and from venerating any hero hateful to you.

Grant me meekness. Grant me sacrifice. Grant me humility. Grant me to love as you do. Grant me your own sweet spirit. Grant me you.

Amen

Lord, I Am at Peace:
This Christmas Too, Mine Eyes Have Seen You

LUKE 2:28–33

> Simeon took up the child Jesus in his arms and blessed God and said:
>
> "Lord, now lettest thou thy servant depart
>   in peace,
>   According to thy word;
>   For mine eyes have seen thy salvation
> Which thou hast prepared in the presence of
>   all peoples,
>   A light for revelation to the Gentiles,
>   And for glory to thy people Israel."
>
> The father and the mother marveled at what was said about the child.

WHEN I COME TO DIE—Oh, let me die like Simeon.

I, too, have been a watchman, waiting for your coming. I knew the promise of your word. In your word was all my hope. But I sought to see you with my own eyes; so I stayed awake, watching, watching for your coming. O Lord, my soul waited for you more than they that watch for the morning; more, I say, than they that watch for the morning.

I heard it said among the disciples: "Blessed are the eyes which see what you see"—and I wanted so to be blessed! It was your voice among the disciples, saying: "For I tell you that many prophets and kings desired to see what you see, and did not see it, and to hear what you hear, and did not hear it"(Luke 10:23–24).

I myself, I had heard. Sermons and personal declarations and the assurances of many believers, I had heard. But I had not seen. And I yearned, O Lord, to see your salvation.

I prayed, "Come!"

With the Spirit and the Bride I prayed, "Come!"

Since I was *him who hears*, I thundered, "Amen! Come, Lord Jesus."

Such was my Advent thirst and all my hunger: "Come."

And then you did, O Lord! You came!

My Advent has been fulfilled in Christmas, and I see you!

Again this year that great and mighty wonder—a Virgin bearing an Infant—has seized my heart with its glorious love. You came into the world. You've come into *my* world! You came once, surely: two thousand years ago. But that has caused your coming still, daily, daily, morning by morning, for people like me.

And so I celebrated the feast of your Nativity this year with the softer passion of gratitude, and that—the gratitude itself—was proof of your presence.

"Blessed are the eyes which see what you see," you said to the disciples. And what *had* they seen? In sequence, the same three things that I have seen (Luke 10:17–22):

1. The effective power of your name in their mouths: "Even the demons are subject to us in your name!" they said, and you said: "I saw Satan fall like lightning from heaven. Behold, I have given you authority ... over all the power of the enemy."

I, too, have experienced in material fact the salvation of your name. For your contemporary disciples prayed for me, and I was surrounded by your love and the demons did not possess me. Those who believe in you uttered your name for my healing, and though the pain continued, it was changed. Satan could not use it to tempt me. Pain no longer dominated me, for you shared the pain, suffering it with me. Mine eyes have seen you: you have come.

2. And you said, "Nevertheless, do not rejoice in this, that the spirits are subject to you; but rejoice that your names are written in heaven."

There has grown in me this year again a genuine joy, O Jesus. A personal, deep down, inexpressible joy. Joy after loneliness. The joy of new relationship: for I am yours and I am God's. My name is written in the Book of Life.

3. Then you thanked the Father that he had "hidden these things from the wise and understanding and revealed them to babes."

As a baby myself—more needy than able, weaker than strong, foolish from failure, helpless and hungry—I've seen the sheer grace of your love: for I should be dead, but I live! I should despair, but during this Christmas too I've known moments of genuine peace. This cannot arise from me. It has to come as a gift from the Source of Life and Truth and Light and Bread and Love. It is visible proof of you.

Moreover, I have used your name among the Gentiles, and even now I see what light you are for them! My words became your angel to all peoples, testifying that you are the root and the offspring of David, the glory of Israel, the bright and morning star.

> *When I come to die, O Jesus, let me die*
> *   like Simeon.*
> *We, who watched for you, whose eyes have*
> *   seen salvation—*
> *Let us die in peace, according to your word.*
>
> *Amen*

The Story:
The Sorrow of Mary, His Mother

LUKE 2:34–35

> *Simeon blessed the parents and said to Mary the mother of the child:*
>
> *"Behold, he is set for the fall and rise of many*
> *in Israel*
> *and for a sign to be spoken against*
> *(and a sword will pierce even through*
> *your own soul)*
> *that the inmost thoughts of many may*
> *be revealed."*

UNDER SUNSHINE in the Court of the Women, Mary has allowed an old man to take her baby from her arms. The baby didn't cry. Neither did she herself protest. Together they watched the face of the ancient figure as he sang of his own impending peace.

Rheumy eyes, drizzled with emotion and old age; eyelids involuntarily winking against the sunlight; thin lashes, heavy pouches of long thought and longer expectation, Simeon declares this child to be the Salvation of God for all peoples—and Mary's stomach flutters with an unspeakable joy. The weird delight of all these natal days.

She loves her baby. She loves those who love him too. And this old man's fierce singing is in perfect harmony with all the songs still playing in her heart: Gabriel's, Elizabeth's, her own, the choral angels'. Yes, her tummy flutters, and she's grinning like a silly lass, and she doesn't mind.

Simeon finishes that song of peace. He lowers his looking and smiles upon the young mother, and Mary blushes for gladness.

She reaches to take her baby back.

But the old man tightens his grip and does not release him. His brows drop like thunderclouds: ferocity returns.

Mary grows tense.

The baby's eyes switch back and forth from the near and grizzled man to his mama. His smooth face wrinkles with bewilderment.

Mary puts a hand behind herself, feeling for Joseph. She can't turn. She can't rip her eyes from the fierce old man and her little baby.

Suddenly, staring straight back at her, the man speaks. His voice is not peaceful. It shudders and cracks, convinced of catastrophe:

"This child," Simeon growls, "shall be a stone, a great immobile stone, a boulder of judgment among the people."

The baby suffers the crush of this old man's passion. His eyes widen with emergent fear. Mary reaches and reaches, but to no avail. In his huge hands Simeon lifts the child above his mother and higher than her arms can go.

"Some of the people," he rumbles, "will trip on this stone and fall and break their bones. Others will build on him remarkable buildings, strong and safe."

Tragedy is the darkness in the old man's eyes. There is no sunshine now. The baby stares down at Mary, panting, panicking.

Suddenly Simeon thunders, "This child will be a sign!"

Jesus jumps and starts to cry.

Where's Joseph? Mary spins round, scanning the crowds in the Temple courts. *Joseph! Joseph, where are you?* She cannot find her husband.

"A sign!" cries Simeon. "A sign the people will despise! Dispute! Impugn! Deny! But a sign which is God among them, so their own actions will give them away.

"Woman, woman," the old man whispers with such deep sorrow that Mary is drawn straight back to his face. She shivers. He says, "Your son shall reveal the thoughts of the hideous hearts—"

He lowers the child. Jesus is crying. Baby tears roll down his face.

But Mary does not immediately reach for him. Simeon's moist eye is bent on her, now, as if she were suddenly his daughter, and he, her father, heavy with parental sorrow. Indeed, sorrow is flowing from him for her—for *her*—in a terrible flood.

"Woman?"

Mary swallows, stands erect, draws her chin back, straightens her shoulders.

Simeon says, "You, too."

She nods. She saw the sentiment even before he uttered it.

"A sword will pierce your own soul through," he whispers. "And when it is withdrawn, all your affections, all your mother-emotion shall pour forth in a river, love and grieving intermingled."

Mary says nothing. She does not even nod.

The baby has ceased his sobbing.

Simeon takes an aged step forward and joins the child to his mother again, for a while, for a little while. He turns toward the Court of Israel and lumbers away to make his own departure.

And here is Joseph, standing beside her. Mary turns and presses her face into the robes of Joseph's chest. She cannot hug him. She's holding the baby. But she bursts into great, loud, heaving sobs, so he puts his arms around them both and pats her back. He keeps patting her back.

Poor Mary: she doesn't even know if Joseph knows why she is crying now.

There blows a colde wind todaye, todaye,
The wind blows cold todaye;
Crist suffered his passion for mannes salvacion,
To kepe the cold wind awaye.

(Middle English Lyric, annonymous)

Lamb of God, pure and holy,
Who on the cross didst suffer,
Ever patient and lowly,
Thyself to scorn didst offer.

All sins Though borest for us,
Else had despair reigned o'er us:
Have mercy on us,
    O Jesus.
    O Jesus.

(Nikolaus Decius, 1531)

PART NINE

The Two Kings

The Story:
Herod the Great and Greatness

MATTHEW 2:1–2

> *Now, after the birth of Jesus in Bethlehem of Judea—in the days of Herod the king, behold, wise men from the East came to Jerusalem, asking, "Where is the newborn King of the Jews? For we have seen his star in the East and have come to pay him homage."*

KING HEROD THE GREAT built whole cities during his reign. Two of them: Sebaste in Samaria, which he placed on the site of the ancient Israelite capital and surrounded with a wall two miles in circumference. He settled this city with his own picked people, 6,000 colonists, hearts and hands all loyal to him.

Sebaste was finished twenty-one years before the birth of Mary's child, unto whom the angel promised "the throne of his father David."

Two cities, I say, the second far more ambitious than the first: Caesarea on the Sea, a magnificent city, an impressive port. Herod the King built a theater there, an amphitheater, a stadium, palaces (one for his family, one for himself), forums, basilicas, baths, fresh stone, gleaming white facades, streets as straight as mathematical thought.

What a great king was he!

When after ten years that second city was completed, Herod announced abroad a great festival with which to dedicate and to celebrate his vast accomplishment.

And so it was: "He appointed a contention in music, games to be performed naked, a fight for single combats, fights with beasts, horse races." And from all over the world, great people sent gifts and envoys came to do him homage. "Julia, Caesar's wife, sent a great part of her most valuable furniture . . . the sum estimated at five hundred talents." Ambassadors came and knelt before the King, both to give him gifts and to receive gifts from him. Priests of various religions came likewise. Astrologers. Magi.

"It is related that Caesar . . . often said, that the dominion of Herod were too little for the greatness of his soul; for that he deserved to have both all the kingdom of Syria and that of Egypt also" (quotes from Josephus, *The Antiquities*, Book 16, Chapter 5).

All this took place five years before the birth of that other King who, the angel said, "will reign over the house of Jacob, forever."

Herod built grand buildings, too, in cities old and long inhabited. This is the king who remodeled Jerusalem. He built a fortress north of the Temple, a palace on the western edge of the city, towers of size and strength—and the Temple. Herod rebuilt the Temple, enlarging the Mount, constructing double porches on three sides of the Temple courts, establishing gates between the courtyards—gates beautiful, forged of the golden-silver bronze of Corinth.

How good was this king to the religion of the people!

And to himself as well, since south of the Mount he built a royal basilica more glorious than the Temple itself, a place for his own approaching. Sadly, he was not a priest. He could never enter the sanctuary of the Temple. He could build what he could not enter. Humble Zechariah could enter there. Great Herod could not. Therefore Great Herod built for himself a greater house than the one wherein the Lord God dwelt.

Then one day for no particular reason (he had ordained no celebration nor finished a building project) certain envoys arrived in Jerusalem to do homage to a King. Magi, they were. Astrologers from the East. Star-readers whose profession Rome despised. And Herod was ever beholden to Rome. It didn't matter how well these people might read the natural signs; they meant nothing to Herod.

And he would have dismissed their miserable homage— until he discovered that it was not to him that they had come, but to a *newborn* king.

What other King was there for Jews?

On that day when planets were passing in such close conjunction that their light was brighter than any star—on that same day King Herod the Great was himself passing close to a greatness greater than his. Together they might have made a most miraculous light, wherein one king did homage to another, while that other died for the first.

But you cannot see what you can't define.

Herod neither met nor understood the Newborn King, because that one's kingship was not of the world, but Herod defined greatness ever in terms of the world. Greater greatness than his own must mean greater splendor, greater armies, greater power—and a will to kill its enemies. What else could he do, then, but fear and hate the Newborn?—

—of whom the angel said, "His kingdom will have no end."

But of Herod the Great it must be said that he suffered physical misery and magnificent terrors till his end. For he was still killing potential kings—his own son, Antipater— five days before he died. And then he died.

O Jesus,

Help me, this New Year's Day, to choose the right King for the rest of the year and my whole life through:

I confess, I am too much of the world. My desires run to power and splendor, to cities, those great centers of human creation and the greater kings who control them.

I love you. But I do homage to Herod.

I love you. But I seek the advantage of another king.

I love you, Lord Jesus. But I spend my days, my allegiance and my energies on the laws and the approvals of this visible kingdom.

King Jesus, come! Come as King to me. Batter my heart.

Bend

Your force to break, blow, burn, and make me new.
I, like an usurped town, to another due,
Labor to admit You, but O, to no end.
Reason, Your viceroy in me, me should defend,
But is captived, and proves weak or untrue.
Yet dearly I love You, and would be loved fain,
But am betrothed unto Your enemy.

Divorce me, untie or break that knot again;
Take me to You, imprison me, for I,
Except you enthrall me, never shall be free,
Nor ever chaste, except You ravish me.

(John Donne, 1633)

An Exhortation to Christians: *Do Not Blame the World (The Magi), But Follow!*

MATTHEW 2:3–8

> When Herod the king heard of [the Magi's search for "the newborn king of the Jews"], he was troubled, and all Jerusalem with him.
>
> Assembling all the chief priests and scribes of the people, he inquired of them where the Messiah was to be born.
>
> "In Bethlehem of Judea," they told him, "for thus it is written by the prophet:
>
> 'And you, O Bethlehem, in the land of Judah,
> Are by no means least among the rulers of Judah;
> For from you shall come a ruler
> Who will shepherd my people Israel.'"
>
> Then Herod summoned the magi secretly and ascertained from them the exact time when the star had appeared; then he sent them to Bethlehem with the instruction: "Go, search diligently for the child, and when you've found him, bring word to me that I too may come and pay him homage."

Awake, O Church! Be alert to the comings of God. Do not fall to Herod's error, the error as well of chief priests and scribes. Rather, rejoice *however* the news of the coming of God comes to you, whether from within your communion or from the world and unbelievers!

It's the season of Christmas—holy and commercial, both. Again this year we Christians have lamented the way the pagan world has stolen the spirit away. Increasing is important; decreasing is dangerous. So say the marketers. Selling-to-get defines the season, while giving-to-love is precisely the attitude that businesses prey upon!

The giving of God (who so loved the world that he gave his son) and the tremendous sacrifice of Christ (who gave *up* his godly authority in order, then, to give up his *life* for us) are neither honored nor acknowledged nor understood. The best the world can say of the season is that (Lo!) sometimes humans can be nice to each other.

An annual burst of altruism: what a wonder! "And what a miserable substitute," says the Christian, "to Immanuel, the loving God among us!"

Thus the lamentation of Christians at Christmas. And in the lament, a resentment. And in resentment a possible blindness to greater glories of God!

Yes, of course there is truth to the accusations above. The world demeans most holy things. But if we choose to respond more to the world's action than to God's great act; if we allow ourselves to be angry at the world, then we will be blinded to those miracles of truth and divine revelation that occur *in the world* (where they are miracles indeed, the fullness and the impartiality of the love of God).

We will wrap ourselves in the pride of righteousness ("*We* are the beloved of God!") and cut ourselves off from that fullness of heavenly love which embraces all creation. Worse, we will make bitter enclaves of ourselves and cease to represent the love of God before the world which we have ceased to honor.

We will become Herod and the chief priests and scribes of the story.

For this is still the sequence of the one's coming to God—meeting him, knowing him, believing in him:

1. Wise Gentiles, watchful worldlings, may read in the natural signs of creation certain proclamations of the Deity. God is! God is like this! God is very, very near.

Thus the Magi. They read holy truth in a rising star.

Thus the Gentiles of Paul's day: "For what can be known about God is plain to them, because God has shown it to them. Ever since the creation of the world his invisible nature, namely, his eternal power and deity, has been clearly perceived in the things that have been made"(Rom. 1:19–20; see also 2:14–15).

Thus it is in our day. Nonbelievers have accurate insights into God—*our* God, yes; but by his choosing, their God too.

2. Next, this natural proclamation will seek confirmation in revelation.

So the Magi came to Jerusalem seeking the newborn king, making theirs a sweeping search, for their knowing was neither precise nor particular. Unto them the communications of God had never been direct. But Herod and the scribes *did* have an account of the direct revelation of God, in Scriptures. From the prophets comes the precision and the confirmation the Magi need. Now they know—even if they have not yet *met*—the King.

Even so do watchful worldlings come yet today to the Church, seeking from the revealed word (safe in our keeping?) a spiritual clarity for the divinity they've already experienced.

And here is the heart of the matter: how shall we receive them? If we believe there is no good in a world that demeans our Christmas (our Christ, *our* God) neither will we trust the truth these worldlings bring to us. Scriptures will surely teach them and lead them, next, through their third stage of knowing God. Scripture belongs to everyone. But the issue here is not their success; it is our participation! Will we take that third step too?

3. For the natural proclamation, now confirmed and refined by the revealed word, must now go toward its personal encounter. Without this there is not, finally, believing. Without this there would be no sense of a loving God, for nature shows us only a righteous and mighty God. This:

The Magi went to meet Jesus.

But Herod and all Jerusalem with him were troubled by the Magi's search. And the king received no enlightenment, neither from the Magi nor from the Scriptures in his possession. Instead, he feared that authority might by passing from him to another whom he didn't know and couldn't control. No worship in Herod! He was scheming to keep his power.

Now you see, Christian, who would most suffer our scorn of the world. Not the world. But we ourselves. For, fearing that a God not completely in our keeping must be a false, distorted God, we might not (once again, this year too!) truly go, innocently go, like little children go to meet Jesus.

O Church! Let not your doctrines blind you—nor let the revelation God has given you make you arrogant! For it is you who would miss Christmas, then, and not the world after all.

The star proclaims the King is here;
But, Herod, why this senseless fear?
He takes no realms of earth away
Who gives the realms of heavenly day.

The wiser magi see from far
And follow on his guiding star;
And led by light, to light they press
And by their gifts their God confess.

(*Hostis Herodes Impie*, Coelius Sedulius, 450;
tr. John M. Neale, 1852)

Jesus:

Save me from my bitter criticisms, the fruit of arrogance, the proof of an unrighteous self-righteousness. Let the light that pagans find enlighten me—to draw me from darkness to you and only to you.
Jesus:

Save me from worshiping doctrines about you, and lead me to worship you!

Amen

O Little King:
Receive the Best I Have to Offer You

MATTHEW 2:9–12

> *When the magi had heard the king they went their way—and behold, the star which they had seen in the East went before them until it came to rest over the place where the child was. When they saw that star, they rejoiced exceedingly with great joy.*
>
> *Then, entering the house, they saw the child with Mary his mother, and they bowed down and paid him homage. They opened their treasure-boxes and offered him gifts, gold and frankincense and myrrh.*
>
> *But, since they had been warned in a dream not to return to Herod, they went away to their own country by another route.*

Now, O JESUS, yet before the Christmas season is over, I come.

I come to honor you: the baby you at your mother's knee; the human you, whose flesh is vulncrable to the troubles of this existence; the tender you, whose face reflects the feelings of people around you.

I come to the house where you are. I knock. I find the door unlocked. It swings inward, and at your mother's nod I enter. In the courtyard I find you grinning, playing. You hold a leather ball stuffed with hair as the earth is stuffed with dirt.

I kneel down.

You roll the ball to me.

I roll it back.

You catch it and laugh—and I am transported. You've allowed me to play with you, my Lord, and you enjoy the company!

Now you withdraw to your mother's knee, because those who have come with me are entering too. You grow serious at the sight. Are there too many of us now? Are we too big or too colorful? Too strange? Too needy? Too marked with misfortune and sin?

Ah, child, don't be troubled. It is we who are in awe of you. In your presence we can scarcely breathe. You've come from God, holy in your birthing, holy in your purpose here.

"Here," I say. Though this may be the house of your parents, it is the world of a people lost in darkness, and you have come like blazing light, enlightening the places I live and work, the evenings of my family and the daily round of all my duties. But you, holy Jesus, have come as gently and naturally as a child, so that we *can* approach you without the terror of mortals before eternity.

Don't be troubled by *us*.

We have come to worship *you*.

So now we bow before you. (Let all devout in these meditations bow down now.)

O Christ!—and you raise your little hands.

Even while we worship you, you sweetly receive your due—and you bless us too. We feel the sacred heat. We feel your love as gratitude within our breasts, a speechless, healing heat.

And here, my Jesu joy, I open my treasure box, to give you the best I have, one, two, three:

—Gold, which signifies your Kingship over us. Gold—which is all my wealth, my properties, my worldly possessions—I place into your service, my Lord and King; for my attachment to you is greater than my attachment to things.

—Incense, which signifies your divinity. Incense—which is myself, my hands, my skills and all they can accomplish, my energies and purposes in this life—I offer to you as a living sacrifice, a sweet odor in your nostrils, my Lord and my God. For it was you who knew me before I was born, and you who called me by my name.

—Myrrh, which signifies your death. With myrrh—which is my love, my pure unsentimental love for you—I will anoint your feet in the Lenten season. With love will I, this year on Good Friday, cover you in your grave; and with love I'll await your Easter resurrection! Love sent you to me, my Savior. I have no better gift than to love you back with all my heart.

And now I go again. There are but two days of Christmas left. It's almost time to return to the cold, to the grey labors and long January of our lives.

But I have dreamed the dream of your coming again this year! And I know good from evil, love from greed, truth from deceit. Therefore I will not return to Herod, or any other king of power. Not to arrogance or self-righteousness will I go, but only by the route you've shown me, Jesus: by the Way that you *are*.

Kiss your mother for me.

Grow well into your ministry.

Come, visit me often. We'll talk. I'll pray.

I love you, Lord.

Farewell.

As with gladness men of old
Did the guiding star behold;
As with joy they hailed its light,
Leading onward, beaming bright,
So, most gracious Lord, may we
Evermore be led by thee!

As with joyful steps they sped,
Savior to thy lowly bed,
There to bend the knee before
Thee whom heaven and earth adore,
So may we with willing feet
Ever seek thy mercy-seat!

As they offered gifts most rare
At thy cradle, rude and bare,
So may we with holy joy,
Pure and free from sin's alloy,
All our costliest treasures bring,
Christ, to thee, our heavenly King.

Holy Jesus, every day
Keep us in the narrow way;
And, when earthly things are past,
Bring our ransomed souls at last
Where they need no star to guide,
Where no clouds thy glory hide.

(William C. Dix, 1860)

A Teaching:
As We Return to a Warring World

MATTHEW 2:13–19A

Now, when the magi had departed, behold, an angel of the Lord appeared to Joseph in a dream and said, "Rise, take the child and his mother, and escape to Egypt. Stay there until I tell you, for Herod is going to search for the child to destroy him."

So Joseph rose, took the child and his mother by night, and escaped to Egypt, where he stayed until the death of Herod. This was to fulfill what the Lord had spoken by the prophet: "Out of Egypt have I called my son."

When Herod saw how he had been deceived by the magi, he fell into a furious rage. He sent into Bethlehem and the regions all around it, and massacred all the boys two years old and younger, according to the exact time he had ascertained from the magi.

Thus was fulfilled what was spoken by the prophet Jeremiah:

> *"A voice was heard in Ramah,*
> *wailing and loud lamentation,*
> *Rachel weeping for her children;*
> *and she would not be consoled,*
> *because they were not."*

Now, when Herod died. . . .

Now, then: just before we end these meditations on the coming of the Christ, we are given a series of four snapshots. Each is absolutely accurate and truthful. But they are not all alike. So unlike are they, in fact, that taken together they create a cosmic tension, a world at war.

They speak of the world to which we return after the blessing of these Holy Days.

They reveal the several responses this world had—and has, and will ever have—to Christ.

Our response may be faith and an enduring love. But we can't ignore the responses of others, because the more we love and obey the Lord, the more we become his image, the present "Christ" to which the world is responding!

We return to a world at war. (That's what Lent signifies, and Holy Week and, finally, Good Friday.) But we enter not to fight! We enter in the name of Christ to be his representatives.

Snapshot 1: *Hearing, trusting, believing, obeying, loving.*

Heaven speaks. The angel announces that enmity exists, that it is powerful, that its power can kill, and that its murderous force is focused on Jesus—on good-ness, on God-ness, to annihilate them.

Joseph hears the heavenly word—and then presents us with the faithful response. He neither disputes nor questions the angel's command. He trusts it. He trusts as well the angel's promise to return with better news in the future. So to trust in a promise is faith: complete dependence without complete knowledge. And trusting in a command produces obedience: as the angel said, "Rise, take, escape," Joseph rises and takes his family and escapes to Egypt. He obeys. Word becomes deed in him. With all who obey, he *becomes* the will of God made visible on earth.

And all this Joseph does because he loves the baby Jesus, the Son of God who is given but a short while into his own fatherhood.

Oh, let our return to the world be like Joseph's trip to Egypt, not just in who we are and in what we do, but in our accurate sense of the consequences.

Snapshot 2: *The quality of God's mercy.*

It is never presumed that we should make the faithful response of Joseph without God, without his persistent love. He is one who still forgives us and parents us and teaches us how to walk!

Read in Hosea 11 the full prophecy which Matthew says was fulfilled in Jesus: *Out of Egypt have I called my Son.*

Note that "son" also embraces the whole people of God (to whom Jesus joined himself). See how God's love has raised us up from children to adults. And when we are able to admit our sins, wonder at *God's* response, that he does not punish after all. He forgives.

Snapshot 3: *Fear, rage, violence, death, and the death.*

In this case no one speaks. The people whom Wickedness thought he controlled—they deceive him. And the lack of knowledge, far from producing trust in the wicked one, produces fear. Lack of knowledge is lack of control, and the loss of control threatens his power. And this is wickedness, to love power more than God, to turn power to one's own benefit, to live a life centered on the royal *Self*.

Goodness alone might be manipulated by the royal "I."
But that goodness which is Godness-made-manifest first ter-
rifies the royal "I" and then causes it to rage as at a deadly
enemy—because Godness is selflessness. It is both love and
the willingness to die. It can neither be threatened nor controlled nor manipulated.

What then?

Then it must be destroyed.

So self-centered power turns passion to action. As
Joseph made manifest the will of God, so sin makes its own
will visible on earth, by a murderous treachery.

Herod needn't be Hitler, though. Herod is the parent
who consumes her children because their goodness threatens her. Herod is the businessman who destroys the com-
petition, whether outside or inside the business. Herod is he
who knows no holy Sabbath, who honors no elder, who
breaks covenant with spouses and children and governments
and congregations. Herod destroys reputations. Herod,
who has so much, wants more.

And the innocent die. It is always the innocent who die
(for whatever else they may deserve, they don't deserve to
be killed by the royal "I").

Oh, let our return to the world take another route than
this. Let our response to Christ be confession, not conceit.

For Herod's death is death alone. A lonely death. And
death with nothing to follow, save dying and dying forever.

Snapshot 4: *God's triumph over sorrow.*

"Rachel" weeping for the innocents is "Rachel" weeping for the tribes of Israel when they had been exiled from

their land. Judah had been seized by evil and taken to Babylon, where there was bitter lamentation and no song.

But what followed? God's response! God made manifest his own power and love, beginning with the prophecy of Isaiah, *Comfort, comfort my people, says your God. Speak tenderly to Jerusalem, and cry to her that her warfare is ended, that her iniquity is pardoned ... A voice cries in the wilderness, "Prepare the way of the Lord!"*

And this is precisely what follows for the innocents in our final Christmas story. John shall be that voice in the wilderness, crying *Prepare!* And Jesus shall be the Lord, come to turn suffering into redemption, and to turn dying into life for the innocents, the Josephs and the Marys. *Their* dying shall have good company, and then it shall have an end.

Such is the war. Both its reach and its consequence are cosmic. Go in sweet obedience, my beloved—and though you die, it shall end in life for you.

My God, my Father, make me strong,
When tasks of life seem hard and long,
To greet them with this triumph song:
 Thy will be done.

Draw from my timid eyes the veil
To show, where earthly forces fail,
Thy power and love must still prevail—
 Thy will be done.

With confident and humble mind
Freedom in service I would find,
Praying through every toil assigned:
  Thy will be done.

Things deemed impossible I dare,
Thine is the call and Thine the care;
Thy wisdom shall the way prepare—
  Thy will be done.

All power is here and round me now;
Faithful I stand in rule and vow,
While 'tis not I, but ever Thou:
  Thy will be done.

Heaven's music chimes the glad days in;
Hope sours beyond death, pain, and sin;
Faith shouts in triumph, Love must win—
  Thy will be done.

(Frederick Mann, 1928)

A Benediction:
Christ Is in Us Now

MATTHEW 2:19–23

Now, when Herod died, behold, an angel of the Lord appeared in a dream to Joseph in Egypt, saying: "Rise, take the child and his mother, and go to the land of Israel, for those who sought the life of the child are dead."

So Joseph rose and took the child and his mother, and went to the land of Israel.

But when he heard the Archelaus was king over Judea in place of his father Herod, Joseph was afraid to go there, and being warned in a dream, he withdrew to the district of Galilee. There he went and dwelt in a city called Nazareth, so that what was spoken by the prophets might be fulfilled: He shall be called a Nazarene.

LUKE 2:40

The child grew and became strong, filled with wisdom. And the favor of God was upon him.

T HE "TWELFTH DAY" is also "the Epiphany of our Lord," one of the oldest festivals in the church's year. In Asia Minor and in Egypt it was already being celebrated in the second century.

The verb *Epiphainein* means in Greek, "to show forth, display." When it's used in the passive voice, it means, "to come into light, to come suddenly into view, to present oneself, to appear."

Epiphany celebrates the "manifestation" in this human child of his deep divinity. It shines forth like a flood of light, and "all flesh . . . sees it together!" Even the Gentiles recognize the God-ness of Jesus. The Magi who came from the East—they were Gentiles. They were *our* envoys for the child Christ. And even now they grant us assurance that we have seen King Jesus, and that our worship, too, is received by him as dear and genuine.

So this has been the dawning light of our meditations these thirty-seven days: Jesus.

Jesus, wholly human; Jesus, God among *us*, this place and this day—Jesus *is* the light of our lives and of the world.

No longer need we pray, *Come*.

He has come.

He is here.

The child, Christ: he grows in us.

We are his Nazareth.

Those who sought his life, though they killed him on the cross, failed in the end. He rose. And he dwells in us.

We are his hometown, now.

Within us that child, the Son of God, is growing stronger. Strength itself is growing in us. Can you feel it?

Within us that Word of God grows wise and wiser. Can you sense the holy wisdom now occupying your mind? It's the consequence of meditation, when the object of our meditations is Jesus.

Upon us the favor of God, the same favor God shed upon Mary, rests and increases. Can you see it? Oh, rejoice in the glow!

The Son in us makes children of us all! Children of God. And since "favor" and "grace" are the same, we are the graceful! Rejoice!

But the joy that has grown in us through Advent and Christmas is not mere *happiness*; knowledge has tempered that. Wisdom won't let us like fools demand a simple, giddy happiness. Joy knows suffering and still does not despair. Joy sees the suffering of others and does not turn away, but moves forward in courage, to comfort and to heal.

Jesus is in us now. Therefore:

The strength and the wisdom of God,
The grace and the joy of our Lord Jesus Christ,
The life and the light of his salvation
Be with you all
Now and forever.
Amen.

Enjoy *Reliving the Passion*, the companion
book to *Preparing for Jesus*

Reliving the Passion

*Meditations on the Suffering,
Death, and Resurrection of
Jesus as Recorded in Mark*

Walter Wangerin Jr.

NO STORY HAS MORE
significance than this:
the death and resurrec-
tion of Jesus. But
somehow the oft-
repeated tale of
Christ's Passion can become
too familiar, too formalized, for us to
experience its incredible immediacy.

The meditations in this book, which received a Gold
Medallion Award in 1993, follow the story as given in the
gospel of Mark—from the moment when the chief priests
plot to kill Jesus to the Resurrection. But these readings
are more than a recounting of events; they are an imagi-
nary reenactment, leading the reader to reexperience the
Passion or perhaps see it fully for the very first time.

As only a great storyteller can, Walter Wangerin
enables you to see the story from the inside. Discover for
yourself the wonder of the events as they unfold.

Hardcover 0-310-75530-1

The Book of God

The Bible as a Novel

Walter Wangerin Jr.

HERE IS THE STORY of the Bible from beginning to end as you've never read it before. *The Book of God* reads like a fine novel, bringing a wise and beautiful rendering of the Bible, retold by master storyteller Walter Wangerin Jr.

Wangerin recreates the high drama, low comedy, gentle humor, and awesome holiness of the Bible story. Imaginative yet meticulously researched, *The Book of God* offers a sweeping history that stretches across thousands of years and hundreds of lives, in cultures foreign and yet familiar in their common humanity.

From Abraham wandering in the desert to Jesus teaching the multitudes on a Judean hillside, *The Book of God* follows the biblical story in chronological order. Priests and kings, apostles and prophets, common folk and charismatic leaders—individual stories offer glimpses into an unfolding revelation that reaches across the centuries to touch us today.

Pick up your copy of *The Book of God* at a Christian bookstore near you.

Hardcover 0-310-20005-9
Softcover 0-310-22021-1
Audio Pages 0-310-20422-4
Video 0-310-21068-2

We want to hear from you. Please send your comments
about this book to us in care of the address below. Thank you.

ZondervanPublishingHouse
Grand Rapids, Michigan 49530
http://www.zondervan.com